HENRY MILLER
THE LAST DAYS

A Memoir

by

Barbara Kraft

Copyright © 2016 by Barbara Kraft

Introduction © 2016 by Paul Herron

Edited by Paul Herron

All rights reserved. No part of this book may be reproduced in any form or by electronic or mechanical means, including information storage and retrieval systems, without permission in writing from the publisher, except by a reviewer who may quote brief passages in a review.

SKY BLUE PRESS
San Antonio, Texas

Library of Congress Cataloging-in-Publication Data

Names: Kraft, Barbara, 1939- author.
Title: Henry Miller, the last days : a memoir / by Barbara Kraft.
Description: San Antonio, TX : Sky Blue Press, 2016.
Includes bibliographical references.
Identifiers: LCCN 2016015718 | ISBN 9780988917088
(pbk. : alk. paper)
Subjects: LCSH: Miller, Henry, 1891-1980.
Miller, Henry, 1891-1980—Friends and associates.
Authors, American—20th century—Biography.
Classification: LCC PS3525.I5454 Z7136 2016
DDC 818/.5209 [B]—dc23 LC record available at
https://lccn.loc.gov/2016015718

ACKNOWLEDGMENTS

Correspondence from Henry Miller used by permission of the Henry Miller Estate

Correspondence from Eugene Ionesco used by permission of the Eugene Ionesco Estate

Correspondence from Alfred Kazin used by permission of the Alfred Kazin Estate

INTRODUCTION

It could be argued that it was mere chance that drew Barbara Kraft, a young aspiring writer, into friendship with each party of one of literature's most famous love affairs: Anaïs Nin, and then Henry Miller; yet, upon reflection, it seems it was meant to be.

In 1974 Kraft signed up for a writing course with Nin only months before the discovery of the cancer that would end the famous diarist's life two years later, and Kraft would prove to be a faithful and dependable friend and companion until the end. During this time, Kraft kept a diary detailing the events of her relationship with Nin, which would become the heart of her acclaimed memoir *Anaïs Nin: The Last Days*.

Only a few months after Nin's death, Kraft attended a "Q & A" talk by Henry Miller and, inspired by his dynamism, did a "crash" rereading of much of his work. This rediscovery led to Kraft writing and reading "An Open Letter to Henry Miller" on an NPR station, which Miller eventually heard and admired. Wanting to meet Kraft, Miller invited her to cook dinner for him, and, of course, to engage in conversation with him, a habit Miller developed during his destitute days in 1930s Paris when he arranged to invited for lunch and dinner each day of the week in exchange for good company.

While Miller was no longer destitute, but in failing health, the ritual of dinner and conversation continued. Kraft became one of Miller's sixteen regular cooks, and she developed not only a comradery with him, but a mutually nurturing friendship for the last two years of his life as well.

This memoir is an inside look at the chaos that ruled the famous house on Ocampo Drive in Pacific Palisades, the long stream of people who lived or crashed there, the revolving door of seekers, celebrities, scholars and filmmakers, and how Miller maintained a fulfilling and creative life in the midst of all the commotion. We see the dynamics of Miller's relationships with his family, his young love interest Brenda Venus and those who professed to care for him as his health declined. We discover how some sought to exploit him and how others rose to the occasion when he needed help. It is a highly personal story in which Kraft captures Miller's conversations so perfectly that one can imagine his voice uttering the words.

Henry Miller: The Last Days is a celebration of Miller's indomitable spirit as his body failed him, his rebellion against old age, his refusal to give in, his never-ending submission to the creative urge, his battle to preserve his right to dinner, wine and talk even if it meant superhuman effort. It is the story of how one of America's most celebrated writers could have died alone in a house full of strangers.

After absorbing Barbara Kraft's sensitive and yet bold narrative, one cannot help but have even more respect for Henry Miller's courage and humility, and rejoice in his final triumph.

—*Paul Herron, San Antonio, Texas, May 2016*

CONTENTS

Henry Miller: The Last Days 11

Appendix 169

About the Author 196

Notes 197

Here in my opinion is the only imaginative prose writer of the slightest value who has appeared among the English-speaking races for some years past. Even if that is objected to as an overstatement, it will probably be admitted that Miller is a writer out of the ordinary, worth more than a single glance; and after all, he is a completely negative, unconstructive, amoral writer, a mere Jonah, a passive acceptor of evil, a sort of Whitman among the corpses...—George Orwell, *Inside the Whale,* 1940

Henry Miller: The Last Days

It is not death that challenges us at every step but life. We have honored deatheaters ad nauseum but what of those who accept the challenge of life.—Henry Miller

Henry lived in a disarmingly quiet, upper-middle-class residential neighborhood in Pacific Palisades and I had dinner with him on a weekly or bi-weekly basis for the last two and a half years of his life. I cooked dinner for him when I was there and over those dinners we shared an intellectual and nearly familial intimacy that was far more seductive than his legendary reputation as "the king of smut."

As he told me during an interview I conducted with him on the occasion of his 88th birthday, December 26, 1979, "I'm old-fashioned and I'm glad to be old-fashioned because I think they have misinterpreted my own words. It's true that I gave a good heavy dose but along with it I gave other things. It wasn't sex alone, but that's what they took... It was also needed. It was very necessary. But they have gone overboard now. There's no sense of moderation. Sex is not everything. It's the last thing in a way, in one sense, compared to love. Without love one is hopeless. One can't live without love. It's the spiritual food that we subsist on."

A modest man, surely the most unaffected, unselfconscious human being I have ever met, Henry resided downstairs in the two-story home he bought in the '60s to house his former wife Lepska (they had divorced in the early '50s), their two children, Tony and Val, and himself. And as I came to learn, although there was a buzzer next to his bed, he refused to use it. When he wanted to summon his "secretary"—I use the word skeptically—or someone else currently residing in the house—crashing is the more accurate word—he would call on the telephone: "This is Henry—you know, Henry who lives downstairs." One of the nicest things about Henry Miller was his total lack of affectation, his genuine modesty when he wasn't showing off for visitors—then he could be, and often was, outrageous.

Beset by a multitude of infirmities the last decade of his life, Miller worked as furiously as ever producing several books (among them the three-volume *Book of Friends*) and hundreds of watercolors. He continued to maintain his voluminous correspondence with the world and entertained a seemingly inexhaustible stream of visitors, which included movie stars, people who came to interview him, academics who came to write about him, and film crews eager to document the passing of an era.

Those who came to visit were met by a weathered quotation tacked to the front door under the brass knocker. The quote was from Meng Tse, an oriental mystic:

> *When a man has reached old age and has fulfilled his mission, he has a right to confront the idea of death in peace. He has no need of other men, he knows them already and has seen enough of them. What he needs is peace. It is not seemly to seek out such a man, plague him with chatter, and make him suffer banalities. One should pass by the door of his house as if no one lived there, advising all those who would ring and enter to pass by quietly, leaving to peace and contemplation the man inside, who, having passed his 86th year, deserved both.*

Yet, for the most part, Henry let "those passing" in. Some he performed for, some he insulted, others he beguiled. There was a striking photograph of the young Ava Gardner in his entrance hall. When the lady came to visit in the flesh Henry overheard her chauffeur asking, as they left, where she wanted to go. She responded, "Anywhere. Just anywhere." Henry found that a remarkable answer.

And in August of 1978, Jerry Brown, accompanied by his entire entourage, paid a call at Ocampo Drive. Miller was in one of his wicked moods. Being wicked was a pure delight to him, but he was never malicious. He greeted Brown, saying, "You know, I think politicians are the scum of the earth, next to the evangelists. I can't stand Billy Graham." Henry had a way of benignly saying outrageous things. Having said them he would sit back, a cat pawing at a mouse, a crooked smile playing expectantly around his lips, waiting for the response his words would elicit.

He told me that Brown exploded with laughter and that they went on to talk about Zen and *Siddhartha*, among other things. "He liked my watercolors too," Henry said. "They were spread out on the Ping-Pong table. He stayed two and a half hours. Talked frankly and when he left asked if he could return again soon."

During his lifetime Miller received abundant praise and even more condemnation; certainly his work left no reader indifferent. Norman Mailer, who defended Miller against feminist critics in *Prisoner of Sex*, concluded in his anthology of Miller's writings, *Genius and Lust*, that "with the exception of Hemingway, he has had perhaps the largest stylistic influence of any twentieth-century American author."

"Miller, Miller, Miller...I think we should all be praising you, you are a very good influence," wrote William Carlos Williams in his poem, "To the Dean."

Praise of a different kind came from Karl Shapiro in his 1960 essay, "The Greatest Living Author." He lauded Miller as a "Wisdom-writer...a holy man...Gandhi with a penis." He concluded that "Miller was the only American of our time who has given us a full-scale interpretation of modern America."

In *The Devil at Large*, Erica Jong wrote: "The sex in [Miller's] books was there just as the spirituality was—to awaken, to enlighten, to bring the reader to his senses... Miller's self-liberation is sexual in the cosmic, not the genital sense."

And then there was the esteemed literary critic Alfred Kazin who wrote to me in 1980 following a letter I sent to him regarding his talk during a National Public Radio program during which he described Miller "as anybody and everybody, a meat-and-potatoes man, an ordinary bloke." Miller, as did I, took offense at Kazin's remarks and I sent him a letter to that effect. In response I received a letter from Kazin, dated January 30, 1980:

> Dear Miss Kraft,
> I appreciate your letter very much; thanks indeed. As for Henry Miller, my remarks on NPR were delivered spontaneously, along with remarks

on several other American writers. There is no manuscript.

I am sorry that my piece offended Miller. I think (as he said) that he is a very powerful writer, but a commonplace mind. I don't know why my description of his swimming pool and the lovelies upset him. I saw the pool *and* the lovelies in 1963, when I went down to visit him with Paul Jacobs. In any event, my review of the Jay Martin book said that he is an ordinary bloke. His experience has been torrential. His writing can be positively inspirational to people to whom sex is still the great mystery. But the mind, dear, the mind! Think of Melville, Faulkner, even Mailer: they see things all around, they see life in many perspectives. Henry doesn't.

With thanks for your fine letter,
Alfred Kazin

Time apparently had taken its toll on Mr. Kazin, because in March 1960 he wrote an accolade to Miller in his diary:

> In the Pittsburgh airport yesterday a.m. I finished re-reading Miller's *Tropic of Cancer* and by God was impressed. A poet's book. Miller has real innocence of the eye; he enters with genuine gusto into the dead Paris world of piss and brothels and rotten cheese. He has true good will, and this is why it is impossible in reading not to like him, not to feel exuberant, to enter into the experience of the senses... As Proust says, we "reason" too much

> to avoid letting the object penetrate into our souls. Miller knows how to register this effect of objects on his soul.

Henry died on a Saturday afternoon in his four-poster bed in his Pacific Palisades home, June 7, 1980 at the age of 88, but this story begins when I first heard him speak:

Fall 1977—Saturday, three to five, Henry Miller "Questions and Answers." Five foot-eight, perhaps less, a slight but enduring frame, delicate but tenacious like the white prayer trees of Japan, gray suit (reminding one that he was of the Bogart generation), red-checkered shirt, kerchief carefully folded in lapel pocket, white socks, bedroom slippers, a slender, but sturdy carved cane.

A slow crossing from the wings to the chair, table, microphone, water glass...a crossing slow and labored on the arm of his friend the director Jack Garfein who was moderating the event at the Actors and Directors Lab. Cane in the other hand, but not an "old man." Although his face was wrinkled and his hands purple and heavily veined, still somehow, face and hands and demeanor seemed to defy his 85 years.

I was in the audience that day and I was enchanted, charmed and totally satisfied. Miller was the Miller I had come to know in his books. Wonder of wonders, Miller the man matched the Miller of the page. Rare that. The man and the work are often two very different things. I had been afraid that in the flesh Miller might let me down. Might be but a pale hint of the work, the half moon behind the sun. But no! He and his work fit together like two halves of the same shell. A shell with the luster of the sun, full of light. The naturalness, the straight-ahead and direct prose, the clean

Henry Miller: The Last Days

simplicity, the lack of affectation or pomposity, the affirmation of tone, the humor and wit, the flow of the born storyteller; in short, the unbeatable spirit of the man. All of those qualities that light up the page for me lit up the stage that day.

I was so moved by the talk I went home and began rereading much of Miller's work, which buoyed my spirits, as I was going through a difficult and protracted divorce at the time. So I started reading—*The Colossus of Maroussi*, *The Air-Conditioned Nightmare*, the essay books *Stand Still Like the Hummingbird*, *The Wisdom of the Heart*, *The Smile at the Foot of the Ladder*—to name a few. When I was done I wrote what would became "An Open Letter to Henry Miller," which I read and broadcast over KCRW, the Santa Monica-based NPR station, October 2 and 4, 1977; it was rebroadcast a few months later on the occasion of his 86th birthday, December 26, 1977. My meeting with Miller was the result of this half-hour celebratory radio program, which began:

> Dear Henry Miller,
>
> I am a long time, serious, I mean I've read all the work, and ardent, meaning I love the work, fan of yours although I've never allowed myself the liberty of writing to you. Still, for a considerable time I have wanted to do so. Now comes this opportunity...[1]

What happened next was pure serendipity. Miller had three children, and the eldest from his first wife (there were five wives in all) was also named Barbara. While I did not know her, she and I were both seeing the same therapist at the time. Barbara Miller was seeing him because of her father's lifelong neglect, and I was seeing him because of my imminent divorce. It was the therapist who, unbeknownst to me, gave her the tape of my *Open Letter to Henry Miller* tribute, which she, in turn, sent to her father. Miller wrote her the following letter after listening to the tape:

> December 24, 1977
>
> I listened to the cassette you sent me yesterday and was astounded, overwhelmed. You say this Barbara Kraft is a writer and that she gave this message over the radio. (Was it over the National Public Radio by chance?)
>
> I am extremely curious about this woman. It was an extraordinary appraisal both of me and my work I thought. In fact I am getting several copies of it made (Don't you want one for yourself?) Tell her for me, if you see her again, that even Anaïs Nin could not have done as well as she.
>
> If you have the time send me her address and I will write and thank her. Thank you for sending it to me. By the way your painting won't get mailed until next week probably. Post office too crowded to go inside. Have a good holiday... Love, Dad

Henry's daughter forwarded her father's letter to me and I wrote to thank him for his kind words.

> Dear Henry Miller,
> I am the one who wrote the radio essay—for lack of a more appropriate word—on you and your

work. I am deeply touched that you found my feelings about you appropriate and harmonious. What else can I say to you? It must be obvious that I have read nearly all the work and that I love it. Your words continually sustain and recharge my batteries. Yours is a vision that I strive towards, working to incorporate it in my own peculiarly feminine way into this "being" that I am.

Perhaps I should mention that I was very close to Anaïs during the last three years of her life. I worked with her on journal writing, and the journal I wrote during my time with her was published with a preface by her. She lived long enough to see *The Restless Spirit: Journal of a Gemini*[2] published by Les Femmes in Millbrae, California before she died. It was terribly important to her. She often spoke of you to me and I hope you don't mind my telling you that. It was always with the deepest affection and admiration and a kind of reflective nostalgia.

I know you must be deluged with letters, visitors and so forth and I don't mean to add to that burden. Simply to tell you how grateful I am that you exist and expressed that living in the words, which stretch out a network across the leaf of my existence. Perhaps if we don't meet in this life we shall in another.

January 14, 1978—a postcard from Henry Miller: *Thank you for your good letter. Yes, I'll be happy to see you—soon. Still swamped by the holiday spirit. My best to you! Henry Miller.*

At the end of January I received an invitation from Henry's son Tony asking if I'd be willing to visit Henry and cook dinner for him.

My response was immediate even though the summons struck me as a bit odd. What I didn't know then but learned after successive visits chez Miller, was that Henry had a list of people whom he enjoyed and who came to cook for him. A different face very night. Food and conversation to go with it. The list was long and the "cooks" rotated. All reminiscent of the modus operandi Henry devised to ward off starvation during the Paris years. In *Tropic of Cancer* he describes how he sent letters to fourteen people asking if he might lunch or dine with them one day a week. The lean years were long over, but the style remained.

My first dinner with Henry occurred on February 3, 1978. In retrospect it was a meeting of "getting to know one another." I arrived at 6:45 and was told by Tony that Henry was resting and would be out shortly. He told me to make myself at home and left the room. I put the dinner I had a been asked to bring in the oven to keep warm and while waiting for Henry to appear, I wandered about the house looking at everything...the dining room, the kitchen, a passing glance at the famous bathroom and an in-depth perusal of a large lanai-like room, which is where the majority of his watercolors were hung. The walls were covered with his paintings. All derivative in style—Chagall, Miró, Picasso even—full of joy, exuberance, color, life. What surprised me was the element of fantasy. Everywhere little or large *objets d'art*—pieces of fantasy—the beamed ceiling papered with posters.

The eye never got bored; rather it was overwhelmed. There was too much to look at. There was his dedication to list-making over the years. The visitor was greeted by two in the entrance hall—one citing pieces of music played in the Polish pianist Jakob Gimpel's master classes, which Henry often attended. (As a young man he had studied the piano but gave it up when he married Beatrice Wickens with whom he had his daughter Barbara.) Next to it a list of cock and cunt words—alongside a photograph of a beauteous and young Ava Gardner. Side by side *Gaspard de la Nuit* and tits and ass.

In the dining room there were framed lists of his favorite foods...no vegetarian fare...and an intriguing list of places and people. Places he'd been to like Èze-sur-mer and places he'd not been and wouldn't get to—Timbuktu, the Sahara. On the Ping-Pong table was a list of all the women he had never slept with. A wonderful brew of magic, fantasy, dung and earth. Behind that Buddha-like equanimity lurked a Germanic heritage.

A half hour had passed when I heard a slow shuffling noise in the kitchen and then the famous voice. Leaning on his walker, it was a labored crossing and there he was. Dressed in pajamas and a blue terrycloth robe, fluffy white bedroom slippers and white socks on his feet, Miller continued to charm. Frail, fragile, deaf in one ear, blind in one eye, lame on one side but not broken. Age could not touch him; his spirit was indefatigable and still quite miraculous. The eternal clown, the gentle jester.

The famous croaky Brooklynese voice told me what a pleasure it was to meet me. I went to greet him and shake the thin, veined hand that he slowly extended towards me, his other hand tightly gripping the walker's rail—a slight and bent figure yet full of a quiet vitality.

"I'm honored to meet you," he said as we shook hands. "What you wrote about me is stupendous, wonderful. I can't tell you. It was so perfect, so accurate. I'll tell you, I was almost afraid to meet you. I told my family, 'What if she's an academic?' I'm so relieved you're not."

And then, "Would you like a Dubonnet? I never take cocktails, don't you know? The young people—how they drink, don't you know?"

We sat facing one another at what passed for a dinner table—a redwood picnic table with a checkered cloth over it—talking up a storm. I was rambling on and on with a case of "diarrhea of the mouth," a condition I'm prone to when nervous. I talked way too much, wanting to get everything in, assuming this was my one and only opportunity.

Our conversation flowed like a stream. Lou Andreas Salomé, wrestling (his favorite TV diversion), the absolute, Nietzsche, astrological signs, Ping-Pong, freedom of the spirit, love, the inaccessibility of truth, fabulating (lying), Anaïs, poverty and work.

(I was excited by Miller, not the legend but the person, the man sitting across from me; at 86 he continued to inspire. Turning to Tony, he said, "We could talk all night. We have so many affinities. We are like spirits...we are free spirits." That dinner was a prelude to the many, many dinners that followed over the next two and half years.)

Henry was and remains an avid reader. Someone recently gave him *The Last Temptation of Christ* by Kazantzakis. He liked the work of Kazantzakis but was somewhat skeptical about this book primarily because he has neither affinity nor feeling for Christ. (In a letter I subsequently came across addressed to his friend Wallace Fowlie, Henry wrote, "I am essentially a religious person and always have been. Fundamentally I'm a religious man without a religion. I believe in the existence of a supreme intelligence. Call it God if you wish.")

That night he spoke about Anaïs. "She was the most total atheist I have ever come across."

(Years later, long after both Anaïs and Henry had departed planet earth, I was to meet Anaïs's brother Joaquín Nin-Culmell at an academic conference honoring Anaïs at the Southampton Campus of Long Island University. He invited me to sit next to him at the closing dinner and he told me that before Anaïs died, he had asked if she wanted a priest and her response was "absolutely not," confirming Henry's words about her complete and total atheism.)

Earlier in the day, Evelyn Hinz had been over to interview Henry regarding a proposed Nin biography and he was amused by the fact that finally the true story was going to come out. He was referring to her duplicity. That said, Henry himself took full advantage of Nin's duplicity during the fourteen years of their relationship.

"She would come to Paris three or four times a week from Louveciennes where she lived with her husband Hugo, her mother and her brother. She used to make up the most elaborate excuses, don't you know. It bothered me what she did to those two men. To Hugo and to Rupert Pole. I never understood how she could do it. Hugo saved that family, her family, literally rescued them from the poorhouse. She used to give me money. You know how she'd do it? Every time she ordered a dress she told the dressmaker to add a couple hundred francs extra to the bill. Then she'd give it to me."

Her lies to Hugo bothered Miller but not so much so that he refused to take Hugo's money. Henry was perplexed by Anaïs's duality. With no small bravado he informed me that she never got to him, that he never let her touch him in the way that she affected both Hugh (Hugo) Guiler and Rupert Pole, her lover and companion the last 30 years of her life.

I told him that she had written a letter to Hugo before she died asking for his forgiveness. "She did that?" Henry responded, shaking his head.

"Yes, and he forgave her, writing how meaningful his life had been because of her. How much richer and fuller it had been."

We spoke about the similarity between Hugo and Rupert and that they were both such good men. "Both shared in the legacy she left, Henry."

"You don't say," he responded, shaking his head yet again.

I said I had the feeling that he had been the great love of her life. And he agreed, saying Evelyn told him that Anaïs had said such was the case.

Changing the subject, he said, "Everyone—even my friends told me not to write, to give it up. That I had no talent. But it was the only thing I could do. I failed at everything else. I stuck to it. The important thing is never compromise the work. You can compromise everything else in your life. We all do—we have to. But never compromise the work."

He spoke with enthusiasm about how things were written, "You know, in a dream," and his love of fantasy, of the dream. Contrary to early appraisals of him as "the king of smut," he is a poet of the vernacular but never a coarse poet. His seminal works were written in rage: "It is despair... God, I feel that I am somebody, a force, a necessity—and by some delicious irony, I am planted in a desert on an absolutely futile, ridiculous errand...I am trying to be a man, to speak as a man speaks, and not to leave out anything because of principles of art..."

Rimbaud restored literature to life; I have endeavored to restore life to literature.—Henry Miller

We sat at the table a long time that first evening—until 10 p.m.—Miller sharing his fascination with the tragic love affair between Abelard and Heloise, his appreciation of *Tristan and Isolde*, and Wagner opera in general. He preferred the Dadaists to the Surrealists and compared Breton to the Pope—the rigidity of the doctrine. "You know," he said, "Artaud was 'excommunicated' by Breton. Can you imagine that?"

Before I got up to leave, he asked to see my work. "Not a lot—something representative. Why haven't I heard of you...were you reviewed by the *Times* some time?"

I told him that my first and only book—*The Restless Spirit: Journal of a Gemini*—had been favorably reviewed by the *Los Angeles Times.* "Anaïs urged me to publish the journal and wrote the preface to it."

He excused himself then and asked me to turn out the lights as I left.

I drove home exhilarated, enthused, rejuvenated. I was thrilled that Henry had asked me to send him some of my work. His request had taken me totally by surprise as had his enthusiasm for my *An Open Letter to Henry Miller.*

Barbara Kraft

"It is the best appraisal of me and my work that I have ever seen," he said, adding "don't you know," a Millerism that figured prominently in his speech when he was enthused about something or upset about something, it could be anything..."don't you know?"

Until the last six months or so of his life, "don't you know" was something of a mantra. And now, all these years later, writing about him once again, he comes alive in my memory and that memory brings a smile to my face. It was the first of the many wonderful evenings to come over the next two and a half years. Little did I realize then how intimately involved I would become in his life and he in mine.

On February 3, 1978, I wrote this letter to Henry:

Dear Henry Miller,
Thank you for one of the most enjoyable evenings I have had in a long, long time. Not only is your work an inspiration, you are as well. I am sending you a small bundle of things as per your request—but please don't even begin to think about reading the book *The Restless Spirit: Journal of a Gemini*. I've marked passages in it for you: (1) p. 28 through p. 49—this section for erotic, not pornographic writing; (2) pp. 84-85—in the midst of a depression I tried to write a "Henry Miller" vignette to cheer myself up. You might find it amusing. The rest of the book won't interest you.

Too much crying, whining, ranting and raving over my dragged-out divorce—now two years and running in a state where divorces are generally a six-month affair.

It was necessary for me to have written out the anguish and the sorrow I suppose, but not worth straining your eyes over.

Rather, read the essay on Van Gogh[3]. And a short story on the death of my father, which I think is one of the most powerful things I've done; not beautiful but strong, true.

I need to apologize for my rapid, staccato-like excessive talking when we met. I was both nervous and excited at being in your presence. I wanted to get everything in and of course that was/is an impossibility.

So many things remain that I would like to speak to you about—the path of the light, the power of love and faith versus that much weaker and useless state of hope and so much more.

I enclose reviews (good and bad) and information about myself in response to your query "Why haven't I heard of you?" Also I am having dubs made for you of my play on Lou Andreas Salomé[4].

Should an occasion arise for another visit I would be overjoyed. However, I in no way want to presume upon you. Also please feel no pressure to even look at what I sent. I send it only because you asked me to do so. The important thing—the magic was in meeting you and speaking directly with you. I need no more…

Barbara Kraft

I received the following letter from Miller, dated February 14, 1978:

Dear Barbara Kraft,

I feel apologetic for holding your work so long but my sight is worse than ever and I have had to go at it very slowly. So here are a few things back. The book I haven't been able to look at yet. But first of all let me tell you what a truly remarkable writer you are. The piece on Van Gogh out of this world! The one on your father's death about as strong a thing as I ever read by anyone!

In your curriculum vitae I notice the great part music plays, or has played, in your life. You must know Zubin Mehta's father, don't you? I like him as a human being so much more than his brilliant son. Do you play the piano still? Do you improvise? I almost became a pianist rather than a writer or painter but marrying my teacher finished that idea. I began at 10 and quit at 25.

Today I listen only now and then. Too many other things to do. Scriabin (his 5th Sonata) is my great favorite. With Ravel it's his "Gaspard de la Nuit." Must confess I don't care for Bach at all!

When I do a little more reading I'll invite you over for dinner again. To be honest, I think you are a greater writer than A.N. whom you refer to as your master. You have a better and a stronger command of the language, in my humble opinion. Anaïs was always timid due, I suppose, to speaking Spanish and French first. I never did agree with her, you know, about the importance given psychoanalysis.

By the way, I read (first of all) the thing about HM (Henry Miller) you gave over the radio. It is most excellent. You have lots of fire in you. I forgot to ask what your natal and rising signs are. (Could one be Scorpio?)

My sight is giving out—must stop. I'll pass the book on to Tony after I read the pages you clipped.

Shit! How stupid of me to overlook the subtitle of your book (Gemini). Tho' Walt Whitman was also a Gemini it seems to me there must be other factors to account for your vigor and depth. (My mother was a Gemini and like your father a cold fish. Deliberately refused to read anything of mine—can you imagine?)

Well, enough! All the best to you! Thank you for a great treat!

Henry Miller

Old friends came to visit and cook for him and there were plenty of new ones as well. I belonged to the latter category, as did Brenda Venus who was the last love of Henry's life. A beautiful woman of soft speech with shining black hair that fell just above her waist, Henry credited her with keeping him alive.

"Without her, I wouldn't be able to go on," he told me one evening over a dinner of zucchini Provencal and chicken breasts browned in butter, garlic and lemon. Henry refers to Brenda as his girlfriend, laughs at being

86 and in love with a 31-year-old woman. Is he laughing at himself or is this the survival mechanism that we all employ? The lie to the self? Who cares? As he readily admits, he is a fabulator, lies and embroiders, lives inside the dream, and why not?

Brenda introduced herself to Henry by way of a manila envelope containing "a few actress photographs of myself" that she thought might pique his curiosity. Which indeed they did! As she writes in the book *Dear, Dear Brenda*, "A few days later, Henry sent the first of the fifteen hundred letters he was to write me. We became good friends and, perhaps, even more."

Henry was enchanted and a meeting quickly followed. Brenda was to become the recipient of hundreds of Henry's letters as had been Anaïs Nin before her. A voluptuous woman, deceptively petite at the same time, Brenda possessed a sultry, smoky kind of beauty that coexisted with remarkably delicate features. It was as if aspects of both June Miller (Henry's second wife) and Anaïs Nin had been reincarnated in Brenda Venus.

A Native American born in Biloxi, Mississippi, she had a soft, lulling voice similar to that of Anaïs; there is no doubt in my mind that God sent this particular Venus to ease Henry along the path to his final destiny.

Henry wrote Brenda four or five letters a day and there were many evenings when he would press a batch of these feverish missives into my hand to mail on my way home. He reveled in the pleasure and pain of this his last *affaire de cœur*, fretting when Brenda didn't call or couldn't come to see him, as miserable as a boy in the clutches of Cupid's first embrace.

Henry Miller: The Last Days

He prided himself that he treated her like a queen and often commented with wry bewilderment, "It is only now that I have finally learned how to love a woman. After five wives and when I'm beyond doing anything, now I've finally learned how to treat a woman."

Seeing Brenda to the door in his walker was one of his gentlemanly, twilight gestures. A selection of Miller's 1,500 plus letters to Brenda Venus were published in 1986 as *Dear, Dear Brenda*. Lawrence Durrell, who wrote the preface, describes Brenda as "an Ariel to his [Henry's] Prospero."

Miller said, "Every Sunday Brenda picks me up and we go to the Imperial Gardens on Sunset...you know where they are...they know me there...the woman who owns the restaurant just bought $100 worth of books from me."

I asked which books she had purchased and he said, "*Insomnia* and the second *Book of Friends*." I told him I had liked *Insomnia* and he said it was a favorite of his as well.

"I surprised myself by some of the writing. I got up and wrote most of it in the middle of the night. I wish I would have kept adding to it... It was about Hoki."

Hoki Tokuda was Henry's fifth wife and his nearly crazed and midnight-maddened writing is very much "on the edge." However, being Henry, he never went over that or any other edge.

He spoke about loving his own work. I asked him, or rather stopped him, on the word "loving" and he said, "Yes, I guess I do love my work. I don't often reread what I've done but sometimes when I do, I think, 'Did I really do that?' And then I can't believe that I did it. You know what I mean? And yes, I do love my work. You know, if you don't like yourself how can you like anyone else? You know? When I look into the mirror, I like myself. I love what I see. You know, even if I look terrible, it doesn't matter. And it's not ego I'm speaking of, you know. It's id. I think everything comes from the id."

And on compromise: "The young don't know about compromise. They don't understand it..." He has no affection for the young, believes that the drugs and groupies, the general crashing out scene, is a cop-out. Pure escapism! Henry was quite Germanic under the Buddhist pose of equanimity he would pass off on one. By Germanic, I mean he believed in the value of the struggle and in discipline.

Another thing he had no patience with was government support for the artist. He was convinced poverty brought forth great work.

"When I wrote the *Tropic* books I was a desperate man...I owe everything to poverty. I wouldn't have become what I am without it. You know, I used to beg on the streets. Nearly became a professional. And then one night I quit. It had been a bad night.

"I used to walk uptown as the theaters emptied, you know. Begging! This particular night I didn't get anything. Not a penny. I had a nickel in my pocket for the subway. To go back to Brooklyn. That was it. It was late and had started to rain. Mud everywhere. I was cold and it was an ugly night.

"Then I see this man in tails and white tie in front of me. He must have been to the opera, you know. So I go up to him and he pushes me aside. Walks right past me without a word. And then sticks his hands in his pockets and empties them. Starts throwing—yeah throwing—nickels and dimes and quarters—all his change into the gutter. I was really degraded, humiliated, you know. But there I was, down on my hands and knees picking up the change and wiping the mud off. Right then and there I swore I'd never beg again and I didn't. I've known it all. Every humiliation, every degradation, poverty, starvation!"

This, perhaps, accounted for his dignity. Such experiences, as Nietzsche pointed out, either kill a man or strengthen him.

We also touched on psychoanalysis, which he felt was a crutch, and it is. But as I said to him some people need crutches in order to walk. "Would you deny them the crutches and immobilize them for life because of a physical infirmity?" He thought about what I had said and cautiously agreed, "I guess you're right." It was obviously something that had never occurred to him.

His daughter Barbara, the first of his three children by the first of his wives, was the fly in his ointment of contentment. He readily admitted that he had deserted her and is the cause of much of her trouble, which had taken her to a psychologist. Anaïs told me that she and Lawrence Durrell had been present when Miller received a heartbreaking letter from his then 12-year-old daughter, begging to come live with him in Paris.

"I felt sorry for her," Anaïs said. "Her letter brought back all the pain I had suffered when Papa left us. Henry read the letter and wept. Then he put it aside, took off his glasses and went to the sofa to take a nap. Durrell was there as well. When Henry awoke he had forgotten all about it. He never spoke of it again. That is how Henry was... In all the time I knew Henry and no matter what happened to him, he was always joyous, laughing, full of life and optimism. I never saw him sad or depressed."

When Henry spoke to me of his daughter, it sounded as if he wanted her forgiveness, her absolution—not unlike Anaïs who wanted Hugo's absolution as she neared the end. Perhaps that is what we all will do or try to do as death nears. We want to tidy up the house, put everything in its proper place. We want to be forgiven and absolved. Henry was enormously preoccupied with his daughter's rejection of him as his end approached.

Brenda received a goodly number of Henry's watercolors and lithographs, as did the rest of us who were a constant in his life. When he gave a painting he would apologize at the same time, saying, "In a way I hate to give you this; you'll have to have it framed and it's expensive. Do you mind?"

Henry was a generous man and a thoughtful one, too. One evening as he was signing a lithograph to give to Charles, who tended to him a few hours every day, he stopped suddenly because he simply couldn't remember the man's last name. "You don't think that sounds condescending, do you? To write 'To Charles' without a last name?" Picking up his pen he added "With affection," and said, "Now, there won't be any doubt."

Charles was a tall black man whom Henry was quite fond of. I never did learn Charles' last name and only met him once or twice as he was one of the day people and I was one of the evening ones. Henry liked Charles not only because he took care of him a few hours every day but, and perhaps more importantly, because Charles was not always smiling at him. Henry hated what he called idolaters, strongly suspected academics and detested being fussed over in any way. Charles came in daily to bathe and shave him, and he referred to Charles with affection as his "Negro." He did not mean it with any disrespect. He was quite simply not a man who would have understood the term political correctness and would have taken issue with its implicit meaninglessness.

There was no permanent help in the Miller household, which bumbled along haphazardly day to day. Besides Charles, there was S, Tony's girlfriend at the time and Henry's sporadic secretary, the "cooks," and various itinerant people who slept there for a night or more as they passed through on their way to somewhere else.

Always a pragmatic man in practical matters, this was one of the ways Henry stayed plugged into the world. A different face every night; food and conversation to go with the meal. I never met the other "cooks" as each cook came on a given night.

Over time, Friday ended up being my night. Although Henry and I had enjoyed an immediate rapport and I left thoroughly enchanted, I hardly expected that I would be invited a second time.

However, a few weeks later, on February 23, 1978, I received a telegram from the Miller household: "Henry would like to know if you're available to cook this Saturday evening. Please phone soonest." It was signed "Tony Miller for Henry Miller."

Naturally I responded immediately, although the date was changed to Monday.

Barbara Kraft

As for the cooks, many of whom, but not all, were women, he once had the notion of inviting them to come at the same time to meet one another but decided in the end that it wouldn't work. Henry said, "Women get along with women when they're alone, but when a man is around they are jealous and vie for the attention, don't you think?"

Miller sent me this letter, dated February 24, 1978:

Dear Barbara Kraft,
    Tony tells me you are coming to cook Monday but I must write you today (or never) despite that fact. First off—you are a wonderful writer! I only read the first pages you indicated. Am now on the second batch.
    Let me tell you immediately that, though your styles differ, you are as good as (or better than) A.N. You are more literary. You know the language better and can wield it more effectively.
    (I had to laugh at your imitation of an H.M. line. You steered away from using the obvious word.)
    I begin to realize more and more that women have a language all their own, a feminine language. And they are not afraid of men's words but simply eschew them! Right? A.N. was excellent in that post mortem "Erotica" book, don't you think? What eloquent language."[5]
    Well, I will hold off telling you more till Monday. By the way, did Tony ever send you a signed photo of me? I don't recall signing one. He

says he mailed you the photo. As for his reading your book it will have to be later. It's getting to be like a factory here! (Unfortunately)

Saying on back of the envelope: "It would seem to me that the Japanese woman was put on this earth to introduce a note of beauty and joy in a world which men from the beginning of time have tried to make ugly and unlivable." (Henry Miller)

On March 11, 1978, I wrote the following:

Dear Henry Miller,

I just finished your *My Bike and Other Friends*, which I enjoyed very much. You really do continually affirm the power and glory of the human spirit to wax poetic. As H. G. Wells wrote somewhere, "Every time I see an adult on a bike, I no longer despair of the human race."

I did receive your photo and I put it in my bedroom. It's a wonderfully cranky photo and I've decided that there is no word in current usage to properly describe you. I think only Shakespeare would be equal to the task of finding an appropriate word or term to adequately describe your character. You belong in one of his comedies—well-honed by the experiences of life but not beyond them, ever ready to be tossed about by the elements and, failing that, reliving those that were through "friends" and "bikes" among other things... I think of Falstaff without the belly, primarily a comic figure with depth.

If I did not impair your health with my cooking I would love to prepare another meal for you. I make a wonderful flan, which time prevented me from putting together that day.

All best regards,
Barbara

At the end of March I returned for another dinner and Henry came into the kitchen to visit with me and asked if I minded if he talked to me as I cooked. "Some people mind, don't you know. They get all confused." No, I didn't mind, I was pleased to have his company. That evening I was making a vegetable stew and for dessert I brought the flan that I had made earlier in the day at home.

Again the evening was delightful and stimulating. At 10 o'clock Miller got up and, before kissing me goodnight on my cheek, said, "You must have been in a hurry to leave the last time you were here," he said.

"Yes, I was, as a matter of fact. Why do you ask?"

"Well—you didn't do the dishes. That's part of the job, don't you know? All the cooks do the dishes. I don't have any help, you see, so that's part of the cook's job. You don't feel as if I'm ordering you about, do you?"

"No, not at all." And I didn't really mind, but what he said had given me pause for a moment or two.

He was used to having everyone wait on him, and why not at his age? I remembered Anaïs telling me that Henry once told her that if she ever became ill, he would leave her. And how he worked at his writing while she cooked and cleaned and took care of all the menial tasks on the days she came up from her home in Louveciennes to stay a few days with him in Paris.

Henry told me that he had asked Anaïs to marry him but that she had turned him down, saying, "And what would we live on?"

"I was never wildly in love with her," he said. "I loved her, but it wasn't a grand passion."

And as Henry spoke to me about Anaïs, she too spoke to me about Henry. She once said, "Henry only wanted the joyful moments. The ecstatic times. He once told me that if I were to become ill he would leave me. If I had ever felt that I could rely on him, perhaps we might have ended up together. But it was the other way around. Henry relied on me to provide the necessities. In fairness he never asked me for anything. He was quite happy in his poverty.

"But I couldn't bear to see the way he was living. It hurt me that he didn't even own a typewriter so I gave him mine. I told Hugo that I had dropped mine, that it was beyond repair, and he immediately bought me a new one. In order to give Henry some money to live on I had my dressmaker pad my bills. When Hugo paid them, Madame returned the extra francs to me. Henry didn't want to take them but I insisted.

"No matter what happened to him he was always joking and full of life and joyous. He wasn't frightened by solitude. He found it strengthening.

"Our liaison lasted several years. He was actually very much a romantic. People never understood that about him. I would manage to go up to Paris two or three days a week. Often I would spend the night. I cooked while I was there and cleaned the apartment which was always littered with dirty dishes and ashtrays filled with cigarette butts. We talked books, read our work to each other and made love."

She paused, reflecting for a moment. And then in voice filled with nostalgia, she said fondly, "You know, the first time Henry and I made love, afterwards he turned to me and said, 'Was it okay for you?' Can you imagine that, Barbara, from the man who wrote all those books?"[6]

Henry was reading my book *Restless Spirit*, making comments here and there, and he genuinely seemed to find it interesting.

"I only intended for you to read the sections I marked," I said to him. "It's a diary, you know—not really something that would appeal to you."

"No, it's interesting. I'm reading slowly. It's interesting what you write about Anaïs. That you gave your blood for her and that it was the same type." (Anaïs and I shared type A blood and she had been fond of thinking that my blood was among the 12 pints or more that sustained her during her first lengthy cancer surgery.)

Henry said he was writing a series of vignettes now on all the women he had not slept with. "Don't you think that's a great idea? You know—the ones I didn't have relations with?"

"I'm getting a divorce. From Hoki. You know—the one I wrote *Insomnia* for. We've been separated for seven years and now we're divorcing. She's dragging things out hoping I'll die so she'll get everything. I have my children to take care of. I gave that woman over $50,000—do you know—to start businesses and so forth... I didn't make any money from my work, you know, until I was in my 60s... Hoki has fourteen of my best paintings. They're worth about $2,000 each. That's $28,000 total...

"Are you trying to do that to your husband—take everything?"[7]

He continued, "People nowadays don't fall in love, don't you know? Me—I'm as foolish as I always was. I still fall in love." We talked about how people speak of "relationship" and not of "love"—how careful they are. He agreed with me that human need is germinal to love and deep feelings. "My son Tony—he doesn't have that, or know about that. Need. He doesn't believe in it..."

Speaking about his paintings, of which I have many, Henry said, "I try to be childlike in my painting. When I paint I sing, I'm happy, I'm not serious. I have a good time. But have you ever watched children paint? They're very serious. Intent. Not at all like what we think of as childlike. It's serious business to them."

Another of his observations that evening included, "Those who do more than is asked of them are never depleted. Only those who fear to give are weakened by giving. The art of giving is entirely a spiritual affair, don't you know? In this sense to give one's all is meaningless for there is no bottom...and while I tried to write the truth, I cannot. No one can. I lied—not big lies—but small ones."

The night ended with his telling me that he had a great-grandmother whose name was Barbara Kraft. So he said—could this be true or was this another of his charming fantasies? Magic, fantasy, dung and earth chez Miller, 86 years old in Pacific Palisades, California, USA.

His dear friend Alfred Perlès wrote in his book on Henry that "Miller is fully aware of the problems of the world at large but he refuses to be sucked into the maelstrom. He knows that it is impossible to save the world. He even questions if it is possible or advisable to save oneself."

Henry's mantra—not that he would have used that word—was, "Live simply and wisely, forget, forgive, renounce, abdicate."

June 4, 1978: I went to Henry's on Friday night. So much has happened since then that I can hardly retain any of our dialogue. I cooked and had dinner with him and drove home feeing gay, happy, a little high from the wine but more than that, inspired by our conversation.

I was sailing down Valley Vista, radio blaring—Ravel's *Bolero* was on and admittedly I was speeding and, alas, sailed right through a boulevard stop. It must have been around 10 p.m. Immediately red lights flashed all over the place. I stopped and was confronted by two towering policemen with large flashlights trained on my face, blinding me to everything except their relentless yellow glare.

"License...registration...you went through a boulevard stop...you know that...you were speeding as well...we have to give you a citation for that...have you been drinking...get out of the car, please...put your toes on this line, tip your head back and close your eyes."

I thanked God at that moment for all the years of doing the tree in yoga. I did not swerve or waft about in winery flumes. My toes held to the line; my body was resolute. And I freely admitted to everything. "I'm just a single, lone woman. You really don't need to shine those lights in my face."

I put my hands up to show them that I was not concealing some dangerous weapon. And, "Yes, I was speeding; yes, I went through a boulevard stop; yes, I was drinking...I had wine at dinner...mea culpa...but please, I beg you, don't give me a ticket. Not tonight. I'm going through a terrible divorce and I've had enough trouble for one day." And amazingly, they did not give me a ticket. They must have been feeling beneficent or something.

"We really should cite you. Okay. You owe us a cup of coffee."

They let me go, but followed me all the way down Valley Vista to make certain I stopped at each and every boulevard stop sign. What a helpless feeling. The power of authority. The franchise of the badge. Then when I got home my soon-to-be ex-husband called on the phone and we had yet another terrible argument.

One of the dubious benefits of having been a female friend of Henry Miller was, and remains, the raised eyebrows, the insinuations, the questions: "Were you one of his women? Did he talk dirty to you?"

Henry and I had our obligatory "dirty" talk once only, early on, over a dinner of steamed zucchini, noodles Romanoff, tomatoes Provencal, melon and ice cream. On that evening, I arrived at the Miller house around 6:30 and when I rang the doorbell Henry himself let me in.

"Have you been waiting long?" I asked him. He said no, but he had come to the door because he had a feeling that I was there.

Once we were in the light he asked, "What's that you are wearing? It's so attractive. Have you been to the gym then? It shows (pointing to my bosom) what's that called—décolletage." The "that" was a low-cut, black leotard, black slacks and a black belt studded with brass bangles.

"No Henry, I'm a yoga person, not a gym person."

As I cooked he sat sipping Dubonnet, chatting with me about all the people who came to call, Joan Baez and Bob Dylan among them. He said that Dylan had been rude, turned his back and snubbed him. And Ava Gardner of the front hall picture had asked Henry to escort her somewhere when she left, an invitation he declined.

Henry's heart had been bothering him of late and he was taking nitroglycerin, but halfway through dinner he told me his pain was completely gone. He had received and set aside two books for me. One I already had—the photo book on Anaïs. He had never seen it before and liked it enormously. Particularly the shot of her wading in a stream in Mexico, with her skirt was hiked up, her thighs exposed. She was 70 with a body not a day older than mine.

"Extraordinary," Henry said with appreciation.

The other book was a collection of poems of Greek women poets sent to him by one of the poets. As he doesn't read poetry, and isn't particularly interested in it, he set the book aside for me.

The "dirty" conversation evolved out of a general one that touched on favorite Miller lovers such as Abelard and Héloise and Tristan and Isolde, on Anaïs Nin, on men and women and their differences. I myself prompted the conversation by reading him a short erotic story I had recently written, which led him into a discussion of how a man likes to take a woman.

He was preoccupied with Anaïs and told me about the first time they made love.: "We were drinking in a café, in a corner, and Anaïs was drinking a Spanish wine that was quite potent. We were kissing and one embrace lasted so long that the waiters gathered round to watch. Anaïs said, 'Let's get out of here.' It was her idea, you see. On the way to my place she told me to go on ahead. She stopped and bought a bottle of champagne and brought it up with her already opened.

"I took her the first time standing up. After that we went to bed and did it that way...she was so sensuous, sensual. And like a flower. Always so fresh."

He told me of the time she had come to see him and sat down on a chair, spread her legs wide, lifted her skirt and proceeded to spread herself open for him. "It was like a precious jewel. She was so fragile and fragrant...a jewel, a flower, delicate. No matter what she did."

He was as captivated by the memory of this experience as he had been nearly half a century earlier when it had occurred.

Women perplexed Henry, possessors of a mystery that fascinated and eluded him. While he believed in duality, it was nearly impossible for him to conceive of a woman being capable of pure love. He did not see women as spiritual beings. He remained intrigued to the end that a woman could be simultaneously lascivious and innocent.

The traits he admired most in women were sincerity, beauty, and, as with his friend Blaise Cendrars, innocence. "Women have to be beautiful. I don't just mean physically beautiful, but beautiful in their being. They have to have a soul also, you know. I don't care for beauty raw and nothing behind it. I never did. I was never attracted to that."

He talked about how a man likes to take a woman "any way." "The more bestial, the more exciting...a man likes it standing up against a wall, bent over like an animal..." We discussed the difference between men and women. Men want to fuck and get it off while women want to be made love to, to be held. I read him the story of one of my love affairs and he said, "I'm getting an erection listening to you. That's really erotic."

He then told a typical Miller story. He had been separated by circumstance from his wife for about ten days (a gentleman in his own way, he didn't say which one of the five he was referring to).

"I was feeling horny," he said, "as we had a very satisfying sexual relationship."

He claimed he was at a county fair where he went into a barn that held all sorts of animals. Climbing up on a box he pulled a goat over so that they were on the same level. In the end he couldn't go through with it. "I was afraid someone might come in," he said.

Henry Miller: The Last Days

Fact or fiction? Who knows? As he wrote in one of the essays in *The Wisdom of the Heart,* "Fiction and invention are the very fabric of life. The truth is in no way disturbed by the violent perturbations of the spirit."

On a different note…the novel is dead. Henry didn't like the first structured pages of my journal as much as the erotic scene, got bored, and said it was "too analytical."

"Don't analyze. Action's the thing. Write the action and then comment in between. You have extraordinary insight into the workings of men and women, so use that. Make psychological comments but don't analyze… You can write anything, you know! That first piece you did on me. I was amazed at the completeness and the economy…the thing is to make a total commitment to the page. Single-mindedness. It takes single-mindedness!"

When I left he embraced me warmly, patting my behind and kissing me on my cheek several times. What an invincible spirit.

But the Miller I related to was not the Miller of the *Tropic* books, but the Miller of the epiphanic books that came after, such as *The Colossus of Maroussi* or *Stand Still Like the Hummingbird,* or *Big Sur and the Oranges of Hieronymus Bosch* or *The Air-Conditioned Nightmare.*

As he said in *Big Sur*,

> The longing for paradise, whether here on earth or in the beyond, has almost ceased to be. Instead of an *idée-force* it has become an *idée-fixe*. From a potent myth it has degenerated into a taboo. Men will sacrifice their lives to bring about a better world—whatever that may mean—but they will not budge an inch to attain paradise. Nor

will they struggle to create a bit of paradise in the hell they find themselves in. It is so much easier and gorier to make revolution, which means, to put it simply, establishing another, a different, status quo. If paradise were realizable—this is the classic retort!—it would no longer be paradise…

Seeking intuitively, one's destination is never in a beyond of time or space but always here and now. If we are always arriving and departing, it is also true that we are eternally anchored. One's destination is never a place but rather a new way of looking at things. Which is to say that there are no limits to vision. Similarly, there are no limits to paradise. Any paradise worth the name can sustain the flaws in creation and remain undiminished, untarnished."[8]

June 22, 1978: "What are we having for dinner?"

"I thought you might like a pasta and homemade tomato sauce."

"No fish?"

"No. No fish."

"Thank God. All I've been having lately is fish. I'm sick of it."

I told him he was looking well. Considerably better than the last time I had seen him, to which he replied, "Do you know what I've got? It wasn't my heart at all. I've got shingles. Can you imagine that? They've given me cortisone for it and I feel fine. I've had a real spurt of energy and have been painting like mad."

Henry Miller: The Last Days

As he spoke he gestured towards the Ping-Pong table in the middle of the room that overlooks the pool, which is where he paints. The table was covered with the paints and brushes for his watercolors. Several fresh paintings were on it as well as a pile of posters.

"Do you know the most amazing thing happened this week? I was checking my datebook one morning, you know, to see who was coming that day and so on, and I saw 'I quit' in Tony's handwriting. Just like that. When he came in I asked him what does this mean and he said, 'Just that! I quit. I resign from everything. From the business, from being the executor of your will, from everything.'

"He told me he had a job and it was a good thing for him to quit. He wouldn't tell me what the job was. I suspect it has to do with film or television. He wants to write, you know. I didn't ask him anything about the job. I guess he'll tell me when he wants to. He's had one script picked up on option. It'll be good for him to get out of here. To have someplace to go, something to do. I'll manage without him. S will help me. (By now S was Tony's ex-girlfriend and Henry's quasi secretary/assistant/girl Friday.) She can take care of everything. You know, Tony's a Virgo. So picky! Everything has to be just so."

"I fully understand. My soon to be ex-husband is a Virgo. It's a lousy sign."

I asked him about his will.

He said, "Maybe I should do what Picasso did. Let them fight over it. This business of she gets this and he that…in Picasso's case they all got something and he didn't have to worry about it. Maybe that's the answer. Let them fight over it."

I had recently finished reading Francoise Gilot's book on Picasso. Gilot's biography rang true to me but antagonized most men I knew. Reginald Pollack, Val Forslund—both artists—thought it horrible, dreadful and sacrilegious. A woman dare not attack the idol, the great high god. A woman dare not unmask and show the human face, the whims and idiosyncrasies, the vulnerabilities of a "god."

It surprised me that Henry was sympathetic to the book and to Gilot; he proceeded to tell me a story that confirmed the tone of her book. Whether or not the story is true is another issue.

According to Henry, at some point Picasso's son paid a visit to Henry and told him that when he was a child he went into his father's studio to watch him paint. Picasso was working on several canvasses at one time, going from one to the other rather carelessly. He stopped and asked the child if he liked the paintings and he said, "No, Papa, I don't." Whereupon—so Henry's version of the story goes—Picasso jumped up and said, "What! You don't like them?" And then he proceeded to hit the child back and forth across the face. Exit child.

A few weeks later the son was again in the studio and, pointing to a painting, said, "Papa—I like that painting over there. May I have it?" Picasso gave it to him and carried it upstairs and hung it in the boy's bedroom for him. Shortly thereafter the painting was gone, and the son came crying into the studio to ask what had happened to it. "My painting is gone, Papa."

"Your painting," Picasso said. "It wasn't your painting. It was my painting. I only lent it to you and now I've sold it."

Henry Miller: The Last Days

I don't think Gilot fabricated or even exaggerated in her book. The interesting thing is that the book, despite the disparagement of most male artists, Miller being the exception, sharpened my appreciation of Picasso. Henry agreed with my sentiments on Picasso, saying, "You're right. Absolutely right. I don't find any emotion, any feeling in his work."

August 10, 1978: Last night at Henry's I made a crab soufflé that didn't rise all the way. Nevertheless we had a gay evening, drank a lot of wine, and the soufflé was still quite good. With Tony gone, the house has a more positive and peaceful ambiance to it. Henry's spirit enlivens it once again. The Ping-Pong table is covered with a new batch of watercolors—seven or eight. As I watched he numbered one of them 32/78—the 32nd watercolor in 1978.

S and Bill Pickerill joined us for dinner. When Tony moved out S moved into the house to care for Henry. Bill is something of a lost soul. Not harmful or obnoxious. Quiet and sweet and ingratiating, but not cloying. (At the time I assumed he was having an affair with S but it turned out that he was gay and died of AIDS a few years after Henry died.)

Bill is a sort of caretaker on Gordon Hormel's estate (the old Will Rogers residence on Sunset Boulevard in the Palisades). He swims daily chez Miller, however, and Henry keeps the pool heated for him so that he can put in his laps—some 200-250 a day. How Henry and he met, I have no idea. Most likely S introduced him to Henry. That said, I'm relieved that Bill is there every day and have told him that if there is ever a problem in the house to call me and I'll come immediately. (That day was to come by the fall of the year.)

At Hormel's Bill lives in a Lady Chatterley-style caretaker's cabin. The main house is a bizarre place. The cottage is charming and cozy—a sort of log cabin—one good-sized room with a fireplace, small kitchen, and small bath. Very California West. The main house is a weird blend of logs and plate glass—California Kitsch. It is a pastiche of past and present owners—one motif plastered on top of another. Red-velvet flocked wallpaper in the dining room, huge rough beams, low-hanging Tiffany chandelier hovering over a massive round oak table with ten chairs with one place set for dinner. The living room has brocaded walls, blue crystal chandeliers, and flowered, print drapes à la the '30s.

S looks worn for 29, but then she snorts coke among other things. So much wasted life. She seems both captivated by and intimidated by Henry. She lives in one of the upstairs bedrooms.

August 26, 1978: Brenda, whom I have not yet met, is an inspiration to Henry. He truly cares about her. She has an ear infection and called to say that she was better and he was ecstatic and started to paint again like a madman. All seems quite natural and right. Many would call it ridiculous. And indeed one has to catch one's breath. And perhaps it is ridiculous, but it gives Henry so much joy and energy—does it matter that it is ridiculous? And one must admire Brenda Venus's choice of a "paramour" if in name only.

Henry Miller: The Last Days

Henry is quite unabashed and so charmingly intoxicated by this, his newest and last love. He makes no apologies or excuses but is in a wondrous state over his good fortune. Brenda strongly resembles June, Henry's second wife; she is the same type of sensuous, indolent, murky, exotic woman. In the pictures I've seen of her she often dresses in the style of the '30s. A soft, black crepe dress cut low in the front, one leg and thigh suggestively thrust forward, smoky eyes. To Miller she must be the reincarnation of June. In her early thirties, I would imagine, she is so very, very beautiful, and beauty is renewing and uplifting and one of God's greater gifts.

Throughout his lengthy life Miller always had a woman to inspire him. Anaïs, June, the Asian beauty Hoki, soon to be the fifth ex-Mrs. Miller, and now the beauteous Brenda Venus. His first wife and the two in the middle were less than inspiring to him. He told me he was "the cat's paw for women. I'm their meat. Women like me, given a chance."

After Henry died, Brenda did a four- or five-page nude photo shoot for *Playboy*. In one of the captions adjacent to a full-length nude shot of her cupping her voluptuous bare breasts—breasts that any woman in her right mind would envy—she explained, "Why am I posing for Playboy? A lot of reasons. It had to be in good taste. I did it as if I were a Greek goddess, an imaginary creature. I wanted to play it like an actress. I think Henry would be proud." And she added, "The beauty of our relationship was the purity of it."[9]

❖❖❖

August 26, 1978: I saw Henry last night. I feel so at home there, comfortable. His divorce from Hoki was finalized as of last week. He was tired and dropped off several times at the table. I was frightened he might die right there in front of me. Old age—what a curse—if one is alone. Old age is indeed a curse, period!

How wrong I was. Henry is like Henri Matisse who worked with cutouts when he was old and infirm and confined to his bed. Helped by his assistants, he called the paper collages "painting with scissors." And Henry still sits at the Ping-Pong table doing his watercolors.

As Montaigne wrote about Socrates, "Nor is anything more remarkable in Socrates than the fact that in his old age, he finds time to take lessons in dancing and playing instruments and considers it well spent."

Echoing Montaigne, Henry wrote "Once you accept it (loneliness) and think of it as not being lonely but as being alone it becomes acceptable. In fact you can revel in it... Solitude isn't frightening. It's strengthening."

Bill Pickerill is a positive presence in the house. He visits and swims on a daily basis. And despite S's limitations, which are considerable, it still feels more like a home than when Tony was in situ. The flowers are fresh, no more month-old wiltings stagnating in brackish water. The dishes are done when I arrive, the cabinets are all in order and the refrigerator well stocked. Not like before. I hope S's moving in bodes well for the future and I hope this industriousness on her part doesn't wane with time.

Henry Miller: The Last Days

When Tony was here the upkeep was at a minimal level of existence. The house had a cold and lonely feeling. I always felt Henry was at the mercy of a son who deep down simultaneously loved and resented him and very much needed to get away from him.

Henry is determined to solicit support for receiving the Nobel Prize and has written the following note, which he has sent out to a multitude of friends asking them to write a few lines recommending him for the prize.

> Dear Friend, ("Barbara Kraft" has been added to holograph in his hand)
>
> In my attempt to obtain the Nobel Prize for Literature this coming year I hope to enlist your support. All I ask is for you to write a few succinct lines to:
>
> Nobel Committee of the Swedish Academy
> Borshuset 11129 Stockholm Sweden
>
> Please note that the Committee urgently requests that the name of the proposed candidate not be publicized.

"Do you think it looks pushy for me to send those notes?" he asked me.

"But Henry, that's ridiculous. I'm nobody, nothing. If you are determined to go ahead with this idea, you need famous names, scholars."

Henry corresponded with the man who would win the 1978 Nobel for literature, Isaac Bashevis Singer, who urged him to cease and desist. "That's not how it's done, Henry," he wrote. Typically, Henry ignored this advice and did, in fact, send out many letters, including one to the film director Elia Kazan. Shortly thereafter, Kazan's secretary wrote saying that "Mr. Kazan asked me to drop you this note to let you know that as of this day he has written to the Nobel Committee as you requested."

The business of being an infamous and celebrated octogenarian writer soon to die is overwhelming Henry. He's been working nearly 'round the clock the last few days, signing more than 300 books for some store. He also signed the Nobel request letters and is making notes for a new book on Mississippi—most likely this has to do with Brenda. He is also trying to figure out what to do about his paintings.

"When I die do you think the paintings should stay at the Coast Gallery or should they be divided between the children?"

He told me he has hardly slept at all the past week, which explains the catnaps at the dinner table. Is the frenetic burst of work a way to fight back death? Does he feel it approaching? He was quiet last night. It felt as if he was deep inside himself; it felt as if he was beginning to move away from us.

The phone rang constantly while I was there. Requests for interviews, photo sessions. "Everyone wants to photograph me. It's not something I'm eager to do. I don't think I photograph so well anymore."

Bill Pickerill told me that the house, the dinner table, feels much different when I'm there. "Henry relaxes with you. The two of you have a real conversation. It's a circus with everyone else. Henry carries on and gets all wired up."

One of our most interesting conversations was about Emma Goldman whom he once heard speak and whom he credits with being the reason he became a writer. While he eschewed politics in general, he conceded that hearing her speak could be interpreted as an interest in "politics."

"Now of course you could call that politics. I was interested in the anarchist movement. Not in what the world thinks of as anarchists. I think that Kropotkin who wrote *Bread* belonged with the saints, don't you see. Emma Goldman was a marvelous individual who opened my eyes to the world, to life. And changed me from a potential cowboy, which I thought I was going to be, to a writer...I became the writer after I heard Emma Goldman speak. She gave me courage because prior to that I had picked up a little pencil—two or three inches long and a pad—and I tried to write. I sat down in the kitchen and I threw the pencil aside after ten lines, saying I'll never write, I'll never be able to do it.

"And then I met her in San Diego while I was working as a ranch hand, don't you know, and she talked about the great authors of the 19th century, the whole century practically. I was so fired by what she said and her views on freedom—against the political situation. She was fighting for the working girl, the sewing machine girl. *Bertha, The Sewing Machine Girl* was a play way back then. She was putting up a great fight for shorter hours and better pay and they sadly needed it."

Henry was also fascinated by the work of the English woman Marie Corelli whose biography, written in 1850, he was currently reading.

"This is a woman who didn't mention sex in her books and wrote such fascinating books, don't you know. She wrote about the eternal things. I wanted to say for all of you who are not absolutely ensconced in the depths of sex and can't free yourself from it, read Marie Corelli. Read her and get a spiritual lift. She doesn't believe in the church, in religion as it's taught. She's got her own spiritual belief. She's speaking from some region. I'm at a loss to say where it comes from. It's daring, courageous, it's bravado!

"My hero, you know, is Blaise Cendrars, who is the exact opposite of Marie Corelli. I applaud him for his courage. He led his own life, but she led her own life too, just as that other woman, who is that woman who knew Freud and Rilke?"

I told him that he was referring to Lou Andreas Salomé about whom I had written a radio documentary a few years back.

"She was an intellectual, Henry, and had a great saying that I love":

> Of one thing you can be sure
> Life will treat you badly.
> So, if you want your life
> Go, take it!

September 22, 1978: Last night Henry was out of sorts because his hearing was bad and his eyesight impossible.

"I had a terrible fight with Tony last night. Screaming and shouting at one another," he told me. "He doesn't think I should be actively campaigning for the Nobel. He's embarrassed. He's worried about what people will think. The only other person who doesn't think I should solicit it is Isaac Singer. He wrote and told me I shouldn't ask for it. That it's just given. I told Tony I didn't want him to come and cook for me anymore."

October 14, 1978: Miller never ceases to amaze me. The activity of his mind, his continuing interest in learning.

Last night he asked me to find out about Semiramis. Which I did...a mythical Assyrian queen said to have built Babylon and to have conquered Egypt and much of Asia and Ethiopia. She was variously portrayed in different traditions and legends as a home wrecker, harlot and sorceress. Both Dante and Virgil wrote about her and Dante placed her in the Second Circle, Fifth Canto of *The Inferno* along with Dido, Cleopatra and Helen, amongst other entries. All the great female goddesses condemned for their power... There is also *Semiramide,* the opera by Rossini based on her life, a role that the celebrated Joan Sutherland sang.

"My oldest and dearest friend, the celebrated opera singer Marilyn Horne, sang the 'trouser' role of Arsace, commander of Semiramide's armies in one production of the opera."

Henry was interested then in the book that I had brought with me...the *Dictionary of Classical Mythology*, which led to a conversation about mythology. I quoted Ionesco to him to the effect that mythology is the most important thing: that it comes before history, the latter being a pale attempt to live mythology.

No doubt Henry's sudden interest in mythology was prompted by a recently published book written by his friend Bert Mathieu: *Orpheus in Brooklyn: Orphism, Rimbaud and Henry Miller.*

We moved on from Semiramis to my impending divorce, which I frequently discussed with him.

"Now you're in for it, Barbara. You're one of those women. You're really in for it now." I didn't know what he meant at the time but I was soon to find out.

Truth is respect. I mentioned this to Henry. "When you wrote about whores—in a funny way—your words were an acknowledgement in a way. Do you know what I mean—that truth is respect and in that sense, truth is equality?"

"I think you've got something there," a pause during which he scratched his head as if in thought and then repeated, "I think you've got something there, Barbara."

October 27, 1978: Last night Henry told me I was his favorite guest. This, needless to say, pleased me immensely. The stories we tell one another. He's started to write a play because he wants to show that he can still shock the world.

He announced, "I heard that in order to win the Nobel I'm supposed to kiss up to this one and that one. That the prize is very conservative and discreet. I said, 'None of that. Then I don't want it,' so I started to write this play. It starts out with an actress coming on stage who announces to the audience that she has the greatest cunt in the world."

"I have this acquaintance that did just that, Henry. She's an actress and was taking a singing class. The instructor told her to think of something that would give her courage and a sense of herself before she went on stage and started to sing. After her performance the instructor asked her in front of the audience and class what she had thought of because her performance had been so good. She responded: 'I just kept saying over and over to myself: I have the greatest cunt in the whole world...I have the greatest cunt...'"

Henry said, "My God. You don't say. What a story."

Our talk moved on to abortion, as I was writing a play on abortion at the time—at the Huntington Library in San Marino where I was what they call a Registered Reader.

Henry told two stories of his own:

"I used to go out on Saturday in Brooklyn with a friend of mine who got paid to drop a shoe box or a cigar box containing a fetus off the bridge into the ocean. He got $25. That was a lot of money in those days."

And on a more personal level...

"I came home one day to find my first mistress lying on the couch, her legs dangling over the side and blood streaming down her legs. I knew what had happened. She had aborted our baby. When I came in she told me to go look in the bureau drawer. I knew immediately what I would find. I called the doctor then and he came over and cut the fetus up into little pieces and flushed it down the toilet. It didn't all go down and the damn thing backed up. It was a boy child. My first-born son..."

Bill Pickerill told me that Tony takes great exception to the story and resents Henry telling it because of the allusion to the fetus being the "first-born son."

It was a night of trading stories. I told Henry about the drama of the divorce and he urged me to write it. "You've got to write that story. It's terrific. Don't write it as a short story. Make it a little book. You know—a small book. It's a terrific story. He won't let you alone even now…"

"The truth is we won't let one another alone, Henry…I'm as guilty as he is…"

November 16, 1978: At dinner with Henry last night the conversation drifted again to my imminent divorce.

"Henry, he's changed lawyers five times now during the divorce. It is exhausting. He apparently told his most recent lawyer he wanted the divorce—now three years running—filed as quickly as possible so that we could both remarry."

"You've got to take a chance, Barbara," Henry advised. "You've got to. It's inhuman what he's doing to you. Destroying you inch by inch. One big blast would be one thing and it would be over. But this is inhuman."

Henry gave me the name of Brenda's lawyer and told me to use his name to get an appointment. He also said I should try for a Guggenheim and that he'd write a letter for me. Alas, with so much turmoil in my life, I never got around to pursuing either of his suggestions.

He spoke then about love and how necessary, how vital it is to be in love. "You know," he said, "you've got to take a chance, you've got to expose yourself to the hurt but also to play the game and maintain the mystery."

S told me that Henry mopes and frets over Brenda just like she and I mope and fret over our "loves." He says it's all part of it—the pain and the pleasure. The not knowing. The hurt. He relishes it all, accepts it all. "When Brenda doesn't call he carries on, miserable as a lovesick boy."

Henry Miller: The Last Days

Henry met Wallace Fowlie, who was to become one of his dearest and oldest friends, through his third wife, Janina Martha Lepska, the mother of his two children. Lepska was a philosophy student at Yale, some 30 years younger than Henry, when they met. It was she who introduced Henry to Fowlie, then a professor of French literature at Yale University.

"She was from Yale and I took her away from Yale to Big Sur," Henry told me. "She was very knowledgeable and literarily inclined—a very brilliant woman and she wanted to help me.

"So I said, 'Help me with my correspondence.' Then it was a mess. I said, 'Try to weed out the stuff that seems unimportant to you. Throw it away. Let's burn it.' So I came home that evening and I asked her, 'Well, did you do it?'

"'Oh yes,' she replied. 'I found so many crazy letters. I burned them all.'

"And I said, 'What? Those are the ones I wanted to keep. The crazy ones. I don't want the letters from the academicians, the professors and all those serious people. I don't give a damn about those. I wanted them from the nuts.'

"Lepska loved Wallace Fowlie and introduced me to him. And we became great friends immediately. I'm glad you mentioned it. I would love to recommend people to look up his books. Fowlie was an American who became a Catholic through his tutor.

"His tutor was a French woman as I recall. He spoke French well and wrote it well. He was very *au courant* about French literature, especially French poets. He's written on a number of the symbolists. He is a Christian of the first order whom I admire, and I can swallow anything he says."

After their initial meeting circa 1943 a profound friendship ensued, which resulted in a two-volume correspondence between Henry and Michael Fraenkel published by Carrefour in London in 1939 with subsequent editions in 1943 and 1963.

They called the correspondence *Hamlet Volumes I and II.* Using Hamlet as their point of departure, the letters reveal the sharp clash of personality between Miller and Fraenkel and serve to give dramatic form to the underlying theme, which is "the crisis of consciousness." The letters were an original and bold attempt to examine the modern problems of existence in its ultimate terms and to fix Hamlet's dilemma in a contemporary frame of reference. Before he died Henry gave me the book.

December 4, 1978: Over dinner last night Henry spoke about meeting Sherwood Anderson once, who told him that "as soon as a story came back rejected I'd immediately put it in another envelope and send it out again. Until finally something was taken. Persistence is the thing."

And he actually found time and energy to read *The Politics of Abortion: An American Entertainment*[10], my play.

"You're so imaginative. Did you really think that that all up in two days? I don't think I could do that. I never could do that..."

"Well, I might have thought it up in two days, Henry, but it took much longer to write it."

Bill Pickerill, who was with us that evening, corrected him by saying, "What about *Just Wild about Harry*?"

"Well, that's true," Henry responded thoughtfully. "I wrote it in two days because I was starving and it kept my mind off the fact that I didn't have anything to eat."

Turning to me, he said, "You're possessed. I can see that. It's awful, isn't it? People used to envy me my inspiration. I hate inspiration—it takes you over completely. I could never wait until it passed and I got rid of it... You have a brilliant mind."

December 20, 1978: I finally met Brenda Venus last night. I had dinner at Henry's and he asked if I would mind if she came over and joined us "just to see how you are."

I didn't quite understand what he meant by that but, of course, I was eager to meet her as well. And he certainly didn't need to ask my permission.

She is a stunningly beautiful woman. 32 years old. Can Brenda Venus really be her name? Hmmm! Although she does qualify for the word Venus, being one. She has the same overall tone as June except for the aura of decadence and self-destruction that emanates from pictures of the latter. Brenda resembles the pictures of her physically but has a freshness and vitality not present in June.

Brenda's introduction to Henry was a series of presumably nude pictures she sent him. Someone in the house also told me that occasionally when she visits, she walks around nude for Henry's pleasure. Whether or not this is true, I have no idea. But it is certainly harmless and would have given Henry great pleasure if such were the case.

Brenda was in "contact" with many famous men. I learned this years later in the early '80s when I was reporting for *Time* magazine. The bureau was trying to reach Kareem Abdul-Jabbar to do a short item on him for the magazine's "People" page. The reporter who was assigned to the story kept trying to reach Abdul-Jabbar through his manager with no success and was sent off on another assignment.

I was given the story and told to give it one more shot before the weekend. I called and left a message with Abdul-Jabbar's manager and forgot about it as I didn't expect to get a call back. However, that evening to my surprise, the phone rang around 10 o'clock.

And it was not Kareem Abdul-Jabbar's manager; it was Kareem Abdul-Jabbar himself. "Is this the Barbara Kraft who knew Henry Miller?"

"Yes, but how in the world did you know that?"

He responded, "I take dance lessons and do aerobics with Brenda Venus."

And that's how I got the interview no one else was able to get.

For all her exotic beauty Brenda seems very much an American woman. She claims she teaches ballet and is an aspiring starlet. I think so much of what a person is shows in the voice. One can easily shield the eyes but rarely does one think to try to disguise the voice. Her voice is ebullient with soft nuances of delight and spirit shot through. Like a fine silk shimmering in the light.

I can fully understand Henry's wonder in her. A joyous spirit not yet fixed into a tired mold, pliant and lovely, eager to absorb from him. She is like a gentle tide breaking on the shore of his years and experience. The sound of their voices drifting into the kitchen like a soft, pulsating mist. And while she might very well associate with famous men, she certainly does not have much to gain from her relationship with Henry. Do I over-romanticize? Most likely!

Marcel Duchamp was the most civilized man I have ever met.—Henry Miller

January 1979: Henry was in great spirits when I next saw him a few days after the New Year and we sat at the table until nearly 10 p.m. On his birthday, December 26, 1978, KCRW re-broadcast the program on him, which contained my *Open Letter to Henry Miller*. Again last night he praised the *Letter* as one of the best things written about him and his work.

"I was in ecstasy when I heard it, Barbara. Ecstasy! I tell you it was the best thing I've ever heard. Can you get me several copies? We seem to have run out of the ones we had."

He told me that a female colleague who shall go unnamed recently sent him a university publication containing an article of hers—"A Novel Triangle: Anaïs Nin-Henry Miller-Otto Rank." "I stayed up until midnight writing her a letter—a strong one. I ended up telling her there were gross inaccuracies and that the whole thing was literary poppycock. She sounds like an idolater to me. I can't stand that."

He spoke about going to see the psychoanalyst Otto Rank in Paris in the '30s. "I went to see him once because Anaïs wanted me to. He asked me to come back again—not 'because you need it but because I'm lonely.' He had no friends. He fell in love with Anaïs and rumor has it that his death was actually a suicide because of her."

Henry was very fleet of tongue that evening. Next came a commentary on his friend Irving Stettner's little magazine called *Stroker*.

"I love writing for them," Henry said. "I love writing for a magazine that nobody reads. It's in the ghetto of New York. I call it the ghetto. I think it still is. Second Avenue and St. Mark's Place. Now this little magazine is my supreme delight. This is almost like Saint Francis taking the vow of poverty. You know, I have spoken a lot about my poverty and the value of poverty. But I never adopted it or espoused it as did Saint Francis. I wasn't being poor to work out God's will or imitate Jesus Christ. Maybe I had additional suffering going through my role as an artist. It's quite different than going through it as a saint, do you know what I mean?

"To beg as a saint is a thoroughly different thing than begging as an artist. As an artist you are humiliated to the depths, to the core of your being, by this lack of money to just live, just to survive…

"I write for Irving gratis. And with great pleasure. I write letters that he can print. I don't have to write anything else for him. He told me people are reading it more now that I'm writing for him. Only thing is he wants me to help him edit it."

He told me that he saw Stettner as "a sort of liberated man. He's Jewish, but like me—I'm a gentile, not a Christian, and he takes his religion that way too. But he's a man of great enthusiasm, great spirit."

Like Henry, Stettner also paints watercolors. Describing him as a combination of the artist and the poet, Henry said, "He's always cheerful. Always optimistic. Though he has nothing. He's really living the life of a divine beggar in the slums... He's a delight in this world of ours which is lousy, corrupt, filthy. He's a man of spirit, without money and who's navigating beautifully."

I knew the magazine because Stettner had sent me a copy. "I read it with great trepidation, Henry. You had letters in there describing some of the cooks who came to dinner. Things like 'they bored me to death.' I was terrified I'd find my name among them."

"Barbara, if I wrote about you I'd write gloriously."

He told me that evening that the only book he wrote that was truly inspired was the one on Lawrence. "I used to put up my hands and say stop! I can't get it down fast enough. My hand ached from writing so fast. The other books flowed but the one on Lawrence was pure inspiration."

It was a wonderful night for me. I feel at home there. Like I belong. There's no strain. By now, we're old friends. It's easy, entertaining, stimulating and so warm. I love Henry's easy, unassuming, humble manner. He never pontificates...well, sometimes he does go on. But he does not invite or tolerate "worship." Quite the opposite! He laughs at it, ridicules those who come to worship at the "shrine."

January 17, 1979: Last night over dinner, Henry and I discussed ruthlessness, single-mindedness, vision, Tolstoy, and loneliness versus aloneness.

When he got up from the table to go to his room, he suddenly looked at me and said: "Barbara, I've never given you one of my watercolors, have I? Come pick one out from this table. There're about 25 here. Pick one and I'll sign it for you."

I was overwhelmed and touched and felt like a child in front of the magic castle. I chose a wonderful one—a large, curving female nude that dominates the painting. A plaintive, sad look in the eyes and a graceful body ending in a mermaid's tail. Milleresque figures roam around the white space that remains on the paper. A pair of double figures with quizzical faces—his? Often he does that. In the upper left-hand corner a star amidst other squiggles and at the bottom right side a black-lined eye with lashes. Ironically, the star is a six-pointed Jewish star and shows up in many of his watercolors.

I told Henry that the female nude in the painting reminded me of Anaïs and he responded that after Anaïs died (January 14, 1977) he received a letter from Rupert saying that he had much to talk to Henry about, including his experience of scattering Anaïs's ashes from a plane over the Santa Monica Bay.

Every time I look at the watercolor I feel happy inside. Happy in my friendship with Henry. But more than that. The energy of the painting—the vitality and spirit are infectious, inescapable, demanding that one respond to life. All of Miller is that way. The words and the color all attest to and affirm life.

Therein lies his greatness.

Henry Miller: The Last Days

January 19, 1979: The conversation last night at Henry's was so interesting. His friend Bert Mathieu, a professor at the University of New Haven, joined us for dinner. He's writing a trilogy on the "Three Musketeers of Literature," Henry, Anaïs and Lawrence Durrell. The volume on Henry is already in print—*Orpheus in Brooklyn*.

He is completing the volume on Anaïs (*Freeing Eurydice*) and has just returned from Europe where he met and worked with Durrell in preparation for the final volume.

Interesting man—lively mind and in his fifties, I would guess. Badly dyed hair, henna-streaked with telltale gray playing peek-a-boo. He spoke about the origin of nostalgia. As he explained it the word has to do with a return to the womb. Another word—genius—he says is to give. And therefore genius is always good. I disagreed. Genius, in my opinion, is a primitive force, neither good nor bad; like nature it is quixotic—both transcendent and destructive.

"It's only now that I have finally learned how to love a woman," Henry confided to Bert. "After five wives and when I'm beyond doing anything—now I've finally learned how to treat a woman. Brenda and I have never had a quarrel. In two years not even a cross word."

In January 1979, I wrote Henry the following:

Dear Henry,
 I write to thank you for the watercolor you gave me. It is life-giving. Every time I look at it my heart picks up with the sheer pleasure of the joy

and the light. The vitality and life and love that radiate from it. And a sense of purity—of course, I find that in all your work, as well as in you. I hope I don't offend you speaking so freely but it is nearly midnight and by this time my heart opens up and spills over with love. As the poet Theodore Roethke wrote, "By midnight I love everything alive."

There is purity about you, whatever that is, and surely I don't presume to know other than a striving towards something beautiful and true and intrinsically real. I always feel that in your presence, at your table, in our talks, in your words on the page—and now again in your choice and use of color and image. A real red-red, a bright orange (but then when is orange not bright?), purple, violet, mauve too, green and blue...the fringed eyes, the hermetic scribbling, your double-faced Janus figures, a dove looking up at two stars and the plaintive purple lady with a swirling fishtail. I can't help but think of Anaïs when I look into those melancholy, knowing eyes. It gives me such pleasure and makes me want to scream out, "Let there always be the light!!!"

I think I told you about the "quotes" I have scotch-taped to my mirror—they provide a sort of daily fix—a spiritual brew in lieu of cross and beads or some darker potion. Anyway, I thought it might amuse you to see them since several belong to you. I've put them on a separate sheet.

Lux Aeterna,
Barbara

Henry Miller: The Last Days

Truth lies in this knowledge of the end which is ruthless and remorseless. We can know the truth and accept it or we can refuse the knowledge of it and neither die nor be born again. In this manner it is possible to live forever, a negative life as solid and complete, or as dispersed and fragmentary as the atom. And if we pursue this road far enough, even this atomic eternity can yield to nothingness and the universe itself falls apart.—Henry Miller

January 28, 1979: For first time, I felt uncomfortable at Henry's Friday night. My spirits refused to rise to the occasion and there was a part of me that remained resolutely outside of the conversation—but an observer of it. That part saw an old man, tired but sustained in his existence by the flurry that surrounds him. The house was full of—I hate to write this—the second-stringers. I don't mean it unkindly, for each has his or her place and role to fulfill. The bramble picked up by the tumbleweed blowing across a barren plane. Am I one of them? And they are important, the glue enabling the machinery that is Miller to function as he always has. That is Miller in residence, chez Miller, holding forth.

Still, I felt for the first time the air of joviality was artificial, without real love or intimacy or genuine concern. These people live off him. Linda Lovely—a girlfriend of S's who came to sleep in the spare room upstairs and has never left. There is also someone called Barry in the other spare upstairs bedroom.

And then there is Brenda. At least Brenda infuses Henry with the will to live, to love, to write, and so she perhaps gives more than she gets. The others, however, are less than dilettantes. But then Henry doesn't seem to mind, so why should anyone else?

Me to me—the great loneliness I am feeling at this time… The thing I've feared more than anything else is to be alone. Well, maybe it won't be so terrible. Maybe I'll be happy with freedom. It's certainly something I haven't tried yet. Fear and power rule men's lives; I'm tired of doing for children…meaning men; Henry is the exception.

February 8, 1979: A lovely evening at Henry's last night. Just the two of us for a change. Bert Mathieu sent his book to me and a letter telling me I had made a vivid impression on him. He asked me to send him my book and anything else I had.[11]

Henry told me that his Vietnamese translators had been to see him.

"I asked them if they needed money. If a thousand dollars would help. S wrote out the check. They had crossed the United States and were stunned at the lack of spirituality. 'There is no spiritual element in this country,' they said. They understand religiousness. Do you know what I mean?"

I did know what he meant, having read his *Air-Conditioned Nightmare*, which recounted his three-year odyssey across America upon his return from ten years as an expatriate in Europe.

I left him watching wrestling on TV.

I really dislike the Jay Martin biography. It was written without admiration or appreciation. The "fusion" Martin attempts is false. It doesn't ring true—he misses the spirit of the man—also the tenderness—the softness that must have been there in the early years as well, to say nothing of Henry's incipient humanity. The book is without any semblance of his generosity and humanity, in my opinion.

Magritte wrote, "The basic thing whether in art or in life is presence of mind. Presence of mind is unpredictable, so-called will does not control it. We are controlled by 'presence of mind,' which reveals reality as an absolute mystery."

February 18, 1979: Meshing his fingers together last night over dinner, Henry described our relationship, saying "We have an *entendement*, as the French say."

And we do have shortcuts in the conversation. We go easily from one subject to the next, flitting like bees gathering pollen. A fine feast of words and ideas. What he must have been like 30 years ago, 40. Highly sensitive, even feminine at times, and yet I often feel impaled on his quiet strength, his single-mindedness of purpose and vision.

"What of your husband's vision?" he asked.

"I think I'm being fair when I say this, Henry. He has considerable talent and imagination, but he has no vision. Do you know what I mean?"

"Oh, yes. All the talent in the world is meaningless without a vision. We can have a vision and minimal talent but not talent and no vision."

We got into the subject of words and their meaning, how much richer French is and the Latin-based romance languages than our puritanical English.

"For example," he said, "the word spirit implies piety, whereas the French word—*esprit*—means anything but pious. It means spirit, life, do you know what I mean?"

Indeed I did. There is buoyancy to the French *esprit* that is missing in the word spirit. The latter doesn't bounce back despite the fact that it comes from the Latin *spiritus*—breath. The verb *spirare*: to breathe. The sound of the "t" is dropped in *esprit*, leaving one with the sensation of floating in space, whereas the "t" is an end in itself in the English version.

Henry is so appreciative of the food I cook, of the clothes I wear; I can see how Anaïs fell in love with him. While he always refers to himself as "ordinary," he is anything but; there is much grace in him, both as a person and as a writer. We talked about chaos. He felt I was on to something when I said that I thought art was the ordering of disorder, giving order to chaos. "You've got something there, Barbara."

February 23, 1979: Included in Jay Martin's biography on Henry is an apologia in the form of a letter written by Henry to Lawrence Durrell in response to Durrell's objections to *Sexus*.

Henry refers to his life, which forms the material of the book, saying that he writes thusly not because he is infatuated with his own ego, but, in fact, because he has no ego.

"You should be able to perceive that only a man without ego could write thus about himself... Because I have been 'utterly shameless' in revealing every aspect of my life. I am not the first author to have adopted the confessional approach, to have revealed life nakedly, or to have used language supposedly unfit for the ears of schoolgirls. Were I a saint recounting his life of sin, perhaps then any bold statements relating to my sex habits would be found enlightening—particularly by priests and medicos. They might even be found instructive.

"But I am not a saint... No, I am not a saint, thank heaven! Nor even a propagandist of a new order. I am simply a man, a man born to write, who has taken as his theme the story of his life, a rich life, a merry life, despite the ups and downs, despite the barriers and obstacles, despite the handicaps imposed by stupid codes and conventions. Indeed, I hope that I have made more than that clear, because whatever I may say about my own life, which is only a life, is merely a means of talking about life itself, and what I have tried desperately sometimes to make clear is that I look upon life itself as something good, good no matter on what terms, that I believe it is we who make it unlivable, we, not the gods, not fate, not circumstance."

March 20, 1979: The other night after I told Henry that I had to restrain myself from trying to run over my husband with the car, he said, "Barbara, you'd better stay away from your husband because you'll kill him. He deserves to be murdered. I'd acquit you, but I don't know about the rest of the jury..." And then he said, "You are a woman who commands respect."

I was very touched by his words and it was the most meaningful compliment I have ever received.

March 27, 1979: Henry and I discussed diary writing over dinner tonight.

"I always told Anaïs it wasn't really writing," he said. "The rehashing of everything that has happened." And, "Life always comes first—never art—always life."

April 2, 1979: A lovely and encouraging evening with Henry last night. I went early to swim before cooking dinner.

Over dinner he reminisced, "Whenever I was in love I was in love all the way. I submitted totally. Complete submission—that's the thing."

And he encouraged me about "the" writing, saying "You've got the itch."

I asked him, "Have you had periods when you couldn't write?"

"Yes, that's when I painted...you needn't worry, Barbara, you've got the itch."

On June 3, 1979 Henry wrote me the following:

> Just a word to congratulate you on a marvelous dinner last night. That filet mignon was the tenderist and tastiest meat I have tasted in many a year. This morning I had the pilaf again. Out of this world. You are chef #1 on my list of 16 cooks.

And then when the next issue of *Stroker* arrived:

> Barbara Kraft here last night. Made me the most wonderful filet mignon I ever had anywhere! I have 16 voluntary cooks on my list now. Barbara is the best. And a damned good woman. She's going to send you more stuff for *Stroker*...
>
> Must close now. Good to be alive, even if half blind and deaf.
>
> Henry

Henry Miller: The Last Days

Harry Kahn was a former FBI agent whose territory had been drug abuse. He was also the first Jew in the agency. A highly intelligent if difficult man, more full of gloom and doom than any other emotion, he also wrote and I had taken something of his to Henry. Harry and I met when he answered an ad that I ran in the *Los Angeles Times* for renting my guesthouse. He too was going through a divorce and had a daughter about the age of my daughter. His daughter was living with her mother, and he was very kind to my daughter and she was quite fond of him. Over the course of that year Harry and I became lovers. He was not an easy man, but he was an amazing lover. I took him once to meet Henry. After that dinner Henry said, "He seems to me like a man who's never really been loved...you just have to put it in God's hands, Barbara. That's all you can do."

Letter from Henry to me, June 6, 1979:

> I don't think Stettner has ever published anything in this lingo of Harry Kahn. This language of his, though, very special to a certain class, is real American talk. (To me belongs to cops and robbers more than mere street dialect). I don't know what Irv's reactions will be. I am writing him today about Harry, to reassure him he's not dealing with a plainclothes man. (Excuse me).
>
> Savar told me Saturday what Bert Mathieu's mag did with your article on me. I am waiting to hear from him—since you wrote him a scathing (and much deserved) letter. Somehow I can't believe Bert did this. Believe one of the editors

must have done it. We'll see. But you are dead right—never let anyone print without first reading proof. I have been having similar trouble with my friend publisher Noel Young. It can happen to any one!

All the best!

Henry

June 16, 1979: I took my stepson Patrick to meet Henry today. He was thrilled to be invited and told us about a man he met on a train in France who was reading *Tropic of Capricorn*. Pat and he had a conversation then about Miller, and the man told him that Miller was someone who lived on the margin of society. Henry appreciated hearing that.

I'd cooked at home and Pat carried in the dinner for me...marinated asparagus, chicken breasts sautéed in olive oil and a fettuccine Alfredo. Also a bottle of Pinot Grigio. When we arrived Bill Pickerill was swimming laps in the pool. Pat sat next to Henry at dinner and was amazed to find that Henry was so "very down to earth and just his own person."

Being Henry, of course, he wanted to shock Patrick. Turning to him, he confided, "I'd like to be on the radio one more time. I'd say 'Hello everybody—this is Henry Miller—Fuck all of you!'"

On a more sanguine note, he observed, "You know, Patrick, there are a lot of good women out there but very few good men."

After dinner he signed two of his books for Patrick, who had just graduated from UC Santa Barbara. "To Patrick, Glad you are out of jail, Henry Miller." To which Patrick responded the following day:

Henry Miller: The Last Days

Dear Mr. Miller,

I appreciate the graduation gift very much. It is nice to be out of "jail!" Such order and discipline does not exactly provoke creativity or any profound thoughts about the art of life.

Je vous remercie, et vous envoie mes amitiés.

Patrick

June 24, 1979: I spent my birthday, June 19, at Henry's because I knew that if I was there it would be a good evening, and on one's birthday one needs to be assured of that. Ironically my soon-to-be ex-husband sent me two dozen roses. Crazy, to say the least.

"Warren Beatty is making a film based on John Reed's book *Ten Days That Shook the World*," Henry told me. "He wants to dub in my voice in the New York sections."

He added, "I had a letter from the guy in Mississippi who owns a bookstore there. He liked your piece on me in *Stroker*[12] and said, "She must be very fond of you to write like that about you."

June 30, 1979: I was at Henry's last night. There and only there do I find a dialogue—food for the soul. Henry had asked me to cook for him and Beatty next week but Beatty preferred an intimate dinner for two and understandably so. The film will have clips of prominent people who remember the days when Reed wrote his book. Henry, of course, was one of them. The footage with Henry was shot last week. Henry also tried to get Beatty to use Brenda Venus in one of his films.

July 1979: S phoned yesterday and asked if I would be able to cook that evening. She didn't say why she couldn't do it herself and I didn't ask. As I had no other plans, I went. When I arrived Henry was at the table with two guests—a man and a woman.

"Is someone there? Has someone come in?"

"It's only me, Henry, Barbara. I've come to cook."

"Ah, Barbara. You're cooking. I didn't know that. Barbara, come in. I want you to meet these people."

To them, he said, "This is another young woman who comes to see me now—not the same one as in the pictures. Barbara—this is Ed Holcomb... He has a terrible handicap that he's managed to overcome... He's 97 percent deaf and he doesn't even wear a hearing aid. He went to India and found his master and changed his entire life. I can't tell you how amazing his transformation is. I feel as if I've been given a great gift. He's found enlightenment. He used to be a photographer and he wasn't really getting anywhere and was always broke. He had nothing. His master told him to give that up—to keep it only as a hobby—and to go into business. And it turned his life around. His master also told him that discipline is everything."

And to his guest, "I can't tell you, Ed, how happy it makes me to see you this way. You've given me a great gift. Barbara, do we have enough food for them to stay for dinner?"

"I think we can stretch it, Henry."

In the end they didn't stay, as they had another engagement. But they'll be back the end of September, at which point I'll meet with the woman. She told me that she's traveled all over the world alone.

Henry Miller: The Last Days

"I traveled for about three years. I was a schoolteacher and I quit my job to travel. I went all over North Africa, India, Mexico; I've been everywhere."

An attractive woman—early thirties, rather plain—must have been a flower child in the '60s. Very pleasant with an open face.

Later at home...a man is welded to his image, a player to his role. Yeats. "Man can embody truth but cannot know it."

Late-day burnished July light...

July 13, 1979: For the first time ever, I spoiled the meat when I was cooking for Henry. We were alone and he talked to me so much as I was cooking that I became distracted. The pasta was okay and the flan perfect. I asked Henry the source of "angel" in his "The Angel Is My Watermark."

"It comes from de-evolution, if you know what I mean." I didn't, of course. I had absolutely no idea what he was talking about.

"We started out fully evolved," he explained, "and have de-evolved with time. We were angels before we were men. So now we're trying to get back to that state—to what we were before."

He mentioned the biography on Marie Corelli and found to his great surprise that she reminded him of Anaïs. "One has the sense that neither were ever children," he explained. "They were both born adults and both had an early and unshakable sense of their own destiny...how could a woman like Anaïs be attracted to me? I mean I'm so plain, down to earth."

"But that's exactly why, Henry. You rooted her. She needed your realness, your simplicity and directness. Otherwise she might have flown off into space, given her obsession with escaping anything resembling reality."

Henry commented on being called a poet. "It's the way I've lived my life. The life of the free spirit. Like Rimbaud. He lived the life of the poet. So did Blaise Cendrars. He was a better man than Rimbaud."

Then he told me an extraordinary story about Cendrars when he was dying. "He was a man who wanted to experience life to the utmost, to the fullest. And so when he was dying—he knew he was dying—I forget what it was—some very painful thing, some horrible disease. I'm talking with him, he's sitting in a wheelchair and suddenly I see tears rolling down his face. And I say, 'What's the trouble? What's the matter?' And he says, 'Oh, the pain, the pain. Unbearable.' And then I left him. I couldn't stand seeing the man who was so courageous bursting into tears. And then later I was told that Cendrars refused to take any medicine or drugs to alleviate the pain. He wanted to know what dying was like as well as living. Isn't that marvelous?"

July 23, 1979: A lovely interlude…a mini-adventure… a little romance. Roses and Vivaldi and a man named Wolfgang.

Last night at Henry's I went outside before dinner to cut some roses for the table. There was a car parked in front of the house and a man got out and came up to speak to me. He had soft eyes and speech and manners.

"My friend and I have been to Big Sur where we met Henry Miller's daughter who gave us this address but nothing else. My friend and I are here from Berlin Radio and we were hoping to see Herr Miller. I am embarrassed to approach you in this way but I don't know quite what else to do."

All the time he was looking in my eyes while his voice was caressing my soul. His voice reminded me of Arne, my Norwegian lover of years past; I have always preferred European men to American men. Suspicion and reticence melted away. An attractive man, probably mid-forties, slight build, curly black hair touched with a bit of gray. He asked what I did and I said I was a writer and returned the question—he said "an actor."

"You speak so much softer than a German," I said.

"Well, I was born in Austria."

"That explains it... I can't take you into the house to meet Henry just like that, but I'll give you his secretary's phone number and you could ring her for an appointment. I'll tell her about you and I'll give you my number as well in case you run into any trouble with her."

"How early can I call you tomorrow?" His eyes were deep into mine.

"Any time after ten in the morning."

With that I took my yellow roses and went back into the house and told Henry about the meeting. "But you can have him if you want him, Barbara. Go back out and ask him to come in."

Wolfgang rang the next day at eleven and I invited him and his friend to dinner that evening. In the meantime I arranged to take them to meet Henry after dinner. They arrived at six bringing wine and good feelings. I set the table outside and served an Italian dinner. Prosciutto and melon as a first course and a very light spaghetti in cream sauce followed. Then salad followed by the raspberries they had brought for dessert. We never got to the salad or raspberries because it was getting late and we would have missed seeing Henry.

The three of us piled into my car, a little yellow 914 Porsche that I dearly loved, and set off for Henry's in Pacific Palisades. Wolfgang was good, very good when interviewing Henry. Henry spoke to him about being a worshipper. "You know—I've always had my heroes—my gods."

"And what about the goddesses?" Wolfgang asked.

That stopped Henry for a moment. "The goddesses—I don't know. The goddesses? The only one would be Heloise. Do you know what she said to Abelard? And this when she was a Mother Superior and not a young woman any more. She wrote to him: 'Would that I loved my God as I love thee.' Can you imagine that? Wonderful."

Afterwards we stopped for a coffee at Rive Gauche where Wolfgang's friend Walter interviewed me briefly. We then dropped Walter at his hotel and Wolfgang and I came back home. We drank wine and talked and played like children until I sent him home at 3:30.

An hour earlier the phone had rung, and it was Harry Kahn. Alas, he called from the guesthouse as Wolfgang and I were making love in the living room.

"What are you doing?" he asked.

"What are you doing?" I responded.

"Never mind that. What are you doing?"

"Saying good night to my friend. Then I was going to call you when he left," I lied.

"Don't bother!" Bang went the phone...

Wolfgang: "You are a free woman and you can't ask me to spend the night?"

I wanted to let him stay the night but could not because of Harry. Finally I had to tell him the truth.

"How early can I come back tomorrow?" he asked.

"Noon," I said.

He arrived at my door the next day promptly at noon. And we spent the day in bed making love to Vivaldi. It was wonderful. The day was airy and the leaves sighed brushing up against the sky. In the evening we went to the Village for dinner and then to see *Manhattan*.

A lovely, gentle man. A charming romantic interlude to break the monotony of this long summer and my prolonged, dragged-out divorce. Gently like the softest of kisses on the nape of the neck, like the soft fur on the underbelly of a golden retriever. So unlike Harry. Romantic, loving. Touching, holding my hand, putting his arm around me, running this hands through my newly cut hair. Ruffling it up, delighting in the day. Charming. A charming brushstroke full of light magic. Like Sondheim's *A Little Night Music*. The fantasy that we would meet in Spain and travel together. The reality: the house, my beautiful house on the hill with a sweeping view of the Valley below, goes on the market tomorrow.

My horoscope keeps urging happiness. And Saturday (a week ago) at a wishing well in Chinatown where I threw a coin that ended up in a cup labeled "happiness."

Does that not augur well? Or were all the cups labeled "happiness"?

Henry wrote me the following letter, dated August 1, 1979:

> The other day I had a wonderful unexpected visit from Jack Garfein of the Actors' Lab. Hadn't seen him for months. He is always wonderful to talk to and be with. (Tho' I understand from the fair sex, he is a "lady killer.")
>
> Anyway, I find him an inspiration. During course of our conversation I discovered he not only has an Actors' Lab in N.Y. but also now owns a small new theatre in the new reconstructed section of 42nd St.
>
> And, how could I have done it—I forgot completely to tell him of your play. (He asked to see the copy of Bert's mag with your article on meeting me in the flesh at his L.A. Lab. I know your writing will impress him.)
>
> So I write now to suggest that you write him about your play, would he care to read it, etc. (His great friend is Harold Clurman, theatre critic. Both are reading my play now.)
>
> Here is his home address and telephone:
> Jack Garfein 157 West 13th St. N.Y. N.Y.
> Home tel: 691-9246
> (Don't have serial. See you week from tomorrow.)

All the best!

Henry

P.S. Do you know whose work he is devouring now? John Cowper Powys. Recently read *A Glastonbury Romance*! Crazy about Powys. Puts him above Homer, Dante, Goethe, Shakespeare et alia. Also told me origin of the Lamed Vav biz. (Abraham talking to God after the flood. You know it!)[13]

August 8, 1979: I spent a wonderful evening with Henry last night. Exhilarating, inspiring. As I left I told him what an inspiration he is. "Really—but I'm against everything."

Henry on D. H. Lawrence: "Evelyn Hinz has been kind to edit my Lawrence book. When I was writing the book on Lawrence I got lost. I didn't know what I thought. She says it all makes sense though. She was here to see me. I told her I don't remember what's in it. She said very little had to be done. When I was writing it I was wild about Lawrence. I don't feel that way anymore. I'm not so sure now. But at that time it was Lawrence and Cendrars. They were my gods. Not *Lady Chatterley*. That's the least of his books. *The Apocalypse*—that's the one. Evelyn told me she thought I was a greater writer than I was a man. I told her that was all right. I wasn't offended. That's how it always is, don't you know? It was certainly true of Lawrence. There was a great difference between the man and the writer. He was kind of weak and hanging back as a man. Now Frieda was the one..."

"Was she very beautiful?" I asked.

"No—not beautiful but imposing, regal. She was the one who had all the life in her."

"Well, I think Lawrence probably needed her for that. Did I ever tell you the dream Anaïs had about Lawrence right before she died?"

"No, I don't think so."

"Well, she dreamt that she and Lawrence were standing on a cliff together. Beneath them was a rapidly moving stream and swimming in the stream was Lady Chatterley. And Anaïs turned and said to Lawrence, 'You and I have always been afraid to swim in the stream of life, haven't we?'"

"That's a marvelous dream. But I think Lawrence was a very courageous man in that he wrote against the code of the day. He was the first. He broke all the standards and that was a courageous thing to do. His books were banned."

"What do we write about today, Henry, when there are no standards left to break? When anything and everything goes?"

"That's a good question." He paused for a moment, reflecting. "There's always life to write about. Life is the thing. It's people that ruin it and mess it up. But life itself is wonderful. And you write about yourself. From the depths of the self—that's always valid and fresh."

We then talked about books.

"I don't share your love of Singer, Henry." To which he suggested I read *The Slave* and *The Magician of Lublin*.

And then we moved on to Durrell. "I think you are a much more substantial writer than Durrell. A much greater, more important, more lasting writer. Durrell, in my opinion, is all surface, Henry...wonderful, dazzling, but lacks depth, wisdom."

"But he's a wonderful conversationalist, Barbara. You have no idea."

And then Jack London. "*Martin Eden* is London's most interesting book. London went all over the country speaking at the universities advocating revolution, don't you know." And, "If you want to read sea stories, read Conrad, not London. London's best book is *Martin Eden*. It's autobiographical. His other stuff is about dogs and Alaska. Read Conrad. Not *Lord Jim* but 'Youth' and *Victory.* Also *Heart of a Boy*. I'll have to loan you a copy."

We talked about men and women. He agreed with me when I told him I thought women were stronger than men. "We have to be," I said.

"I think you're right there, Barbara. Men's courage shows up in battles—in war—under fire. But every day is a battleground for women. They're tested every day."

He's been painting again—one large watercolor that resembles Brenda and a few scattered smaller ones. I was in the kitchen when he got up and came out, surprised to see me so early. "I've been swimming, Henry. That's why I came early. To swim in the pool."

"If you don't mind, Barbara, I just want to write something down before I forget it. That's what I got up for." What he wanted to write was an inscription on the Brenda painting. It went something like this: "To Brenda Venus—who illumines..." He asked, "Is that the right word? You know what I mean. Illumines..." Pointing to his head, "It's illumines, isn't it, not illuminates."

I told him I was reading the Durrell-Miller letters and had been amazed at the exchange between them over

Rosy Crucifixion. "I was stunned when I received those letters from Durrell," Henry said, scratching his head, one of his characteristic gestures.

"Did they make you doubt what you had done?"

"No, I knew he was dead wrong."

That is the wonderful thing about Henry. The lack of doubt. The complete embracing of life and all it brings. The sorrows, hardships, disappointments as well as the joys. He takes it all as it comes, as it is, as opposed to someone like my Norwegian lover, a composer who told me, "I doubt everything all the time." Later in life he became the "King's Composer."

We moved on to the work of Thomas Mann and were pretty much in agreement.

Henry: "At one time I loved *Death in Venice*. I was crazy about it. I had a friend who told me to read it aloud and that in so doing I would discover it wasn't a great book. I did as he suggested and discovered he was right."

"I have a lot of trouble with Mann, Henry. I always feel he's hedging, covering all the bets. I don't think he believes what he writes. I always feel the blade of denial in his work. As if his head is riding rifle on his heart. Do you know what I mean? That he denies what he really thinks and feels for what he should think and feel. Look at *Death in Venice*...a man following the sensual, the instinctual, and it all ends up in disaster, death and decay. There is no joy in the work. In the man. He's constantly wrestling with his soul but never seems to come near the light.

"Perhaps it is because he personally experienced the self-destructive potential of love...both his sisters committed suicide, as did his son Klaus who was a homosexual. My very favorite of his short stories are *A Man and His Dog* and *Tonio Kroger*. I very much appreciate his short stories."

August 20, 1979: After dinner with Henry last Friday he gave me another lithograph, saying, as he did every time he gave me one, "I hate to give you this, Barbara, because you'll have to have it framed and it's expensive—do you mind?"

Merrily Carr: "When you see Henry Miller tell him for me that he wrote the best masturbation page there is. It's page 109." I had no idea what book she was referring to. Most likely it was one of the *Tropic* books.

People always need to make reference to the salacious part of Henry's writing, never to the religious, the spiritual, the transcendent. That is there as well as the rest. That is the work that speaks to me. Basically I could care less about the *Tropic* books. I don't think I ever managed to read them all the way through.

August 26, 1979: I took the Irish actress Fionnula Flanagan with me to Henry's Friday night. I prefer going alone. Selfish, perhaps. But I'm too tired these days to "hostess," which is what I do when there is a guest like Fionnula. That aside, what an extraordinarily cultivated woman she is.

Rarely am I envious of other women. In this case I am. She is a very special woman, earthy, lovely to look at, a mass of glorious red hair, sensuous, ripe mouth—a mouth that belongs in a Rossetti painting, a voluptuous body. A measure of her artistry is that on the stage she appears quite tall—5'6" or so whereas off stage and out of the lights she is barely 5'2". I tower over her. The art of illusion is a great asset for an actress.

She and Henry discovered that they both admired the actress Ruth Draper. Fionnula told Henry that she was barely five years old when she saw Draper and was inspired from that experience to go on the stage herself. She told us that her parents were Catholic communists. This, as she described it, was in the 1930s when it was fashionable to be a communist, sitting around drinking wine and talking over ideas in Ireland.

Fionnula is extremely ambitious and immediately offered to come and cook an Irish dinner for Henry, which he avoided committing to, for what reason I have no idea.

He told me, "What I liked about her was her down-to-earth-ness. She's very earthy. She's not an elegant kind of beauty. She just sailed in... I'd like to see her again."

That night, over dinner, she thanked me profusely for my generosity in sharing Henry with her, which made me raise a cautious eyebrow. An endorsement from Henry for her show at the Huntington Hartford—*James Joyce's Women* in which she plays all six roles, including that of Joyce's wife Nora and the fictional Molly Bloom—would not be unwelcome. And she was amazing in the role of Molly to say the least. She appeared stark naked on stage at the end of the play, facing the audience full on with arms spread out to either side. She was absolutely stunningly beautiful in her nudity and majestic as if the epitome of all womankind.

Brenda was there as well that evening, sitting next to Henry, but said little. She and Fionnula found a mutual

Henry Miller: The Last Days

ground of communication, complimenting each other on being beautiful women. And so they were. Brenda with a face out of a Modigliani and Fionnula with a face reminiscent of Botticelli's *Birth of Venus.*

Brenda left while we were still sitting at the table, which prompted Henry to apologize to Fionnula, saying, "I usually walk Brenda to the door. I treat her like a queen. I don't have all my powers about me tonight."

To which Fionnula responded, "Oh yes you do!"

I wrote Henry the following on August 28, 1979:

Dear Henry,

I've been wanting to speak to you about the following for weeks now but didn't as there always seemed to be someone around. So perhaps it is best to write to you. I just wanted you to know that if the present situation with S doesn't work out and you should find yourself needing someone to take her place, I'm available and would love to try it—that is if you think I'd be right. Obviously I hope that S stays on as I know how fond of her you are (as am I), but I thought I should mention this to you just in case there is a change.

I'm also sending you a flyer and the reviews on my book. The *Los Angeles Times* review was excellent, as you will see. They called me a diarist of distinction, writing that I have a "stirring poetic facility" and that I am "a gifted writer"...

And then there was the *San Francisco Chronicle* reviewer who asked, "Would Madame Bovary have committed suicide if she'd taken an

> intensive journal workshop? Probably not. Instead one can imagine her progressing on to Creative Writing I, notebook open, plumed pen quivering."

I was not particularly fond of S, and her care of Henry was shoddy, sporadic and left a lot to be desired. She had told him that she wanted to move out but would come in every day to look after him. My personal situation was worsening as well—given the stress of the protracted divorce proceedings—and I thought perhaps my 15-year-old daughter and I could take over the upstairs of Henry's house. Henry was delighted with the idea. I told him I would need a letter of residency from him in order to enroll my daughter in the Pacific Palisades high school. And this he wrote:

> September 14, 1979
> To Whom It May Concern:
> This is to verify that Barbara and Jennifer Kraft will be living with me at this address as of this date.
> Henry Miller

A few days later, I came to my senses and realized this was a very, very bad idea and told Henry I had changed my mind.

September 1979: Henry and I were alone at dinner tonight. Just the two of us. Henry's dislike of the word commitment: "I was even reluctant to call myself an artist." I said, "I can fully understand that. To describe oneself as an artist seems presumptuous; to describe oneself as a writer is a different matter."

I did an interview with Henry for National Public Radio to be aired in December on the occasion of his 88th birthday. (It was subsequently published in the *Michigan Quarterly*, Spring 1981.)

September 24, 1979: I went to Anaïs's house last night at Rupert Pole's invitation. The occasion was the conclusion of *Diary VII*. Present were myself, the sculptor Val (who had built the tea house for her while she lay dying) and his girls, Renate Druks and Rupert's musician friends who played two Beethoven quartets. Following the music Rupert read the last pages of *Diary VII* and an epilogue drawn from the final diaries. The diaries of pain and music... (Henry thought they were called the diaries of pain and suffering, and added, "But then Rupert changes things to suit himself.")

Diary VII ends in Bali and is the record of Anaïs's last trip there in the summer of 1974. She writes of the Balinese death ceremony by cremation and tells how a white dove is released to symbolize the release of the soul. The Balinese view of death is seen as a freeing agent that permits the transmigration of the soul.

I felt her presence among us and was touched to the core. Tears filled my eyes and I remembered... I remembered what I had found in her beautiful house of glass, in the years spent with her. It all came back because after her death I'd lost it, forgotten it. How she urged me to publish *The Restless Spirit*, saying, "I want you to be free. I don't want you to do what I did."

The strand was broken by her death with the pain and rejection and bitterness that resulted from the publication of the book. I was an outcast in the world in which I had lived for 20 years—a pariah.

One prominent woman, the subject of David Hockney's *Beverly Hills House Wife* and a major patroness of the arts, came up to me at a concert at the Music Center and said, "I'm sorry, but I can't invite you to my musicales any longer because of your husband and the book you published."

Last night the inspiration of Anaïs returned. Once again I sat rapt at her words, her vision, her faith and stamina in the face of unbeatable odds. Her spell remains. Rupert would rob her of her humanness and turn her into a total myth by changing her words, turning phrases ever so slightly so as to mitigate the pain and despair of those last two years. But perhaps that is in keeping with Anaïs herself. For she made herself a myth and did not permit herself the humanizing relief of recording her frailties and weaknesses along with that transcendent vision.

Rupert told a story of how, on one of the many occasions when she was in the hospital, a nurse tried to cheer her up by telling her that one of the benefits of being ill was that one could read. The nurse said, "When I was ill I read all of Marcus Aurelius, to which Anaïs responded, "I've written a lot of books but now I'm afraid I can't live up to them."

These are the types of words and utterances that Rupert edited out, explaining to all assembled that evening that "I don't want to give the critics any ammunition."

As I told Henry, those very words she said to the nurse bear witness to her incredible life journey—from inside the dream cocoon to the world of rueful reality. In one of her late diaries she writes with pride, "I am a realist." She was proud of her ability to finally transcend the introspection that was simultaneously her signature and her prison.

September 26, 1979: Last night at dinner Henry spoke to me at great length about my writing. He had come across two stories of mine that I must have given him at his request—"The Weekend" and "The Day Peace Came Calling." Despite his poor eyesight he had read them.

"I read both the stories, Barbara. The endings are really something. I told Bill, 'Wait until you get to the end…just wait…' But you know, there's something wrong with them, though. Something doesn't ring true. There's a false note somewhere. I'm not quite sure where. In the longer story the woman carries on and complains and makes so much out of nothing. The writing is masterful. It flows wonderfully and the language is perfect. You've got it all. It's masterful. Only you're not giving us enough information. You give the surface, not the substance. In the story you present the husband as a famous artist, only we don't know enough about him to come to that conclusion; also the woman seems weak, acts weak, but really isn't. One has the feeling that she is strong, that she gets what she wants. As I said, you've got it all. Your apprenticeship is over. You're ready to sail forth. Only write from your heart. Always write from your heart and don't hold back.

Write with courage, with all the stops out. Don't hold back! In the stories one feels you holding back…"

And of course he's right on the target. I knew there was something wrong with *The Weekend* and only wrote it because I needed 50 pages to send off to a short-story contest. I knew the story read well even though there was a false note in it. And Henry didn't like the mundane and ordinary tone of the beginning of the story *The Day Peace Came Calling*.

"I did that on purpose, Henry—for the contrast with the later section when the man comes home, goes in the backyard and kills himself."

He still felt that it didn't work. I don't know. Maybe he's right. I was trying to show the ordinariness of life juxtaposed against the drama of the suicide. But everything he said about *The Weekend* was to the core.

Henry on Jesus: "He didn't know what he was getting into. Jesus was no master. A master wouldn't allow himself to be crucified like that."

A soft time…the weeping willows indolent, languid trees astir in the soft breeze…the silent world of small flying creatures illuminated in the late afternoon sun—a thin strand of spider's silk stretching from green blade to green blade…the sun crawling up my thighs…

October 10, 1979: We sat at the table tonight until 10 o'clock. A late evening for Henry these days. We had a great discussion about the words innocence and purity. I argued that purity was a more desirable state than innocence, that it was Edenic, whereas purity implied both experience and wisdom; that no one, man or woman, could or should remain innocent; that ideally innocence evolves into purity of spirit through the transformation of experience and age. Henry himself exemplified what I was trying to express. We never resolved this argument, although we returned to it on many occasions as Henry was loath to part with his romance with innocence.

The subject came up because we were talking about Anaïs whom Henry described as "lascivious" in the sense of being on display.

"But," he continued, "at the same time she was always innocent. Always these contradictions."

"That innocence costs us women a terrible price," I responded.

"That's right," he said. "And that's how it should be. Innocence should cost a lot. Someone once asked Blaise Cendrars what he looked for in a woman, what he most wanted. And do you know what he said—innocence."

"Well, Henry, I'm not crazy about the use of the word innocence because it implies a lack of wisdom. I prefer purity. Because one can have experience and still be pure. One can also have experience and remain innocent, but at what a cost!"

"That's right," he responded, "because to stay innocent one has to put on blinders and not look to the left or the right. I think we have more to discuss on this business of innocence and purity."

Moving on, he said that he always had the feeling of homosexuality about Rupert.

"Ambivalence, you know. But what struck me about him was the feminine. He is very feminine, soft."

Henry also told me that my problem is that I'm prolix. "What exactly do you mean by that, Henry?"

"You talk too much. I have the same problem."

"Well, I agree. You're right. I'm always running off at the mouth. But I think my friends accept me in spite of it."

I said, "They're probably interested in what you have to say."

He told me a funny story in answer to my query about men and their writing about and relating to dogs. "Is there anything in that, Henry?"

"Oh, I think so," he said. "There are times for a man when all he wants is a cunt. Any hole will do—dog, cow, goat. An opening in a fence even...

On October 22, 1979, I wrote Henry the following:

Dear Henry,

In going through my notebook I came across the following, which might interest you until Bert Mathieu sends some heavier stuff. The origin of the word Mephistopheles is a conception of the Greek "Mi Photophilos," which means "He who does not love the light."

I went to hear the Verdi *Requiem* at the Music Center the other night. Glorious music. Giulini conducted and in my opinion everything sounds the same under his baton...slow, no dramatic tension, little contrast...

I'm getting to work on the "book" on Anaïs, combing through my old journals. I've already written so much relating to her death. I used to come home and record our conversations, what she was wearing, how she felt...her dreams, fantasies, fears. Rereading through the weeks and

Henry Miller: The Last Days

months of that last year of her life, I'm struck all over again at what a tremendous privilege it was to have been there, to bear witness. For her death was no random event but rather, in a strange way, a last act of creation that illuminated the whole of her life. I'll write only about Anaïs as I knew and perceived her. Not how others knew her. I'll write with love, compassion, truth. Truth is respect![14]

I'll be there Friday to cook and I am planning to bring Ruth Seymour with me if that is alright with you. She is the general manager of KCRW and responsible for putting so much of my work about you on the air. If not, please ask S to let me know. Until then...

October 27, 1979: This has been an immensely busy week. Wednesday night I went with Noel Young of Capra Press (Henry's publisher) to an awards dinner given by the Southern California Independent Booksellers Association. Miller received an engraved sterling silver bowl as did two women writers who are in their sixties. One of them, whose name I don't recall, writes children's books; the other was Jessamyn West who wrote *The Friendly Persuasion*, her best-known work.

Ruth went with me to dinner at Henry's last night. It was a wonderful evening and Henry immensely enjoyed her company and the conversation; Ruth is nothing if not a scintillating conversationalist and presence.

She told Henry that she had met Noel Young at the awards dinner a few days earlier and Henry asked, "How was he? Was he drunk? He drinks too much and it's beginning to affect his business. You can't run a business that way. Still and all Capra has put out some good things the past few years."

In addition to publishing Henry, Noel did two John Sanford books and Robert Kirsch's book of selected reviews. He also published works by Nin, Durrell, and Patchen as well as *The Oval Lady and other stories* by Leonora Carrington and Jay Martin's biography of Henry, which we all dislike.

It was a wonderful, warm and easy evening; Ruth and Henry had an immediate rapport.

Ruth described herself to Henry, saying, "I'm a romantic, surrealistic anarchist." She told him that she sees the world in political terms. She got Henry to agree reluctantly that, in that sense, he, too, is political.

He responded, "I'm against everything," he said. "I am an anarchist against anarchy."

He asked about Ruth's background and she told him that her father was a Russian Jew and her mother a Polish Jew. Ruth is a first generation American Jew.

"It seems to me that you were obsessed by Jews," she said to Henry. "I'm thinking of the opening pages of *Tropic of Cancer*. And I loved your story *Max and the White Phagocytes*."

Henry said, "I went to look for Max after the war and I couldn't find any trace of him. What do you think happened to him?"

"Oh Henry, you know what happened to him," Ruth answered.

Henry told us that James Laughlin (editor of New Directions) changed the title from *Max and the White Phagocytes* to *The Cosmological Eye* when the book was published.

"He's a prig," Henry said. "He's very wealthy man, owns Laughlin Steel in the East. He came to see me in Paris. At the time I was working on the D. H. Lawrence book and I had all these charts all over the place. He came in and said, 'What's that nonsense?'"

Returning to the subject of Jews and Judaism, Ruth told us about her trip to Israel and her take on the Israelis.

"A few years ago I went to Israel with a group of women journalists. It was a very strange experience. I felt the Israelis were more Israeli than they were Jews. I felt at home with the Palestinians because they were also Semites to me. Everyone had a son studying to be a doctor or a lawyer.

"My father sent me to study Yiddish when I was a child. I later studied at CCNY with the great Jewish scholar Max Weinrich. I said to him, 'I feel I am the youngest person in the world studying Yiddish. When I become an adult will Yiddish still survive?' And he responded, 'Yiddish is magic. It will outwit history.'"

"When Singer accepted the Nobel Prize he did so saying there was no word for weapon in Yiddish," Henry told us. "I thought that was wonderful, just wonderful. I thought that all the papers and reporters would pick that up and put it in headlines. But no one even mentioned it."

Henry brought up the subject of Buddhism, and holding up his wine glass, he said, "We can decide whether we think the glass is half full or half empty."

Ruth responded, "Oh Henry, we Jews don't have a choice. We know that life is a tragedy."

"Jews are a terribly sensual people," Ruth noted, adding, "but with a very deep puritanical streak as well."

She told us that her ex-husband, the poet Jack Hirschman, had been subpoenaed to testify in the obscenity trials on the *Tropic of Cancer,* which were held in Los Angeles at UCLA during the '60s. "Only Jack and the bookseller defended you, Henry, calling you a great writer. Jack read aloud a wonderful passage from one of your books.

"The prosecutor asked him if he used words like c-u-n-t and Jack said, 'Yes, I do.' Then the prosecutor asked, 'And does your wife use language like that?' and Jack answered, 'Yes, in our most intimate moments.'"

Henry can be very sensitive and aware. During dinner he addressed all his conversation to Ruth whom I had put directly across from him in the guest's seat. When dinner was over he said to her, "When Barbara sits across from me we go on all night too... We talk for hours." And then he said, looking at me, "Ruth's so erudite. More erudite than you."

When we left, Ruth said to me: "I can see why Henry likes you so much. It was lovely to see you in the kitchen. It was so homey and relaxed. Warm and comfortable. You're completely at home and know your way around the kitchen, the house," and regarding Henry, "He's so sweet, so courtly, such a gentleman."

November 3, 1979: It has been a very busy week. I found a house in Studio City, made an offer on it and am waiting to hear if the offer was accepted. If I get it, it will be the smallest and least imposing house I've ever lived in, which will take some considerable adjustment. It does

Henry Miller: The Last Days

have two bedrooms and two baths, thank God! And the living room has a wonderful arched ceiling, fireplace and lovely paned picture window in the shape of an upside-down U. There must be a name for it. The down side is that the house was built in 1927.

I had a lovely evening at Henry's last night. Madame Jacqueline Langmann, his Swiss astrologer, was there for dinner. In the '60s she had predicted that the publication of *Tropic of Cancer* in the United States would not fail. She is a fascinating, vital woman, 70 years old but still such a woman. The Europeans seem to be able to maintain their sexuality with age. It has nothing to do with their looks or physical appearance. No, it comes from the inner psyche. They keep their awareness of themselves as women. Although she jokingly referred to herself as an old woman, Madame Langmann is a woman with no age. She remains totally engaged in the world and absorbed in people, ideas, work. It is the engagement with the world that keeps us vital and alive. The challenge of life. She's been married to the same man for 37 years. The conversation alternated between English and French and I was amazed that I was able to understand most of what was said. Languages have never been my forte; my excuse is that I can read music, including a full orchestral score.

"Henry has told me so much about you," she said, looking at me across the table. And to Henry: "*Elle est belle, très belle*"...and later, "She is wonderful." And Henry said, "Like I told you—fluorescent."

Me—fluorescent?

Madame Langmann does astrological and therapeutic consultations. She is an original—unique. About 5'6" with a good figure, she holds herself completely upright and is a handsome presence. She was wearing a blue tie-dyed, well-tailored cotton pantsuit that suited her. She told me she has done yoga most of her life, as have I, which probably accounts for her impeccable posture. Earlier in the year she was injured in Palermo and so, for now, is unable to do any yoga. Someone stole her handbag and knocked her down on the pavement, which resulted in severe head injuries from which she is still recovering.

She told marvelous stories about her practice. "A woman, an older woman came to see me. She complained about her daughter-in-law, saying, 'She can't have children. My poor son.' 'How long have they been married?' I asked her. 'Six months,' she told me. 'But that's nothing at all,' I said. 'And how do you know it's your daughter-in-law's fault? Perhaps it's your son. It can be the man, you know. Perhaps I should see your son.'

"Well, she didn't want that. Here they are married only six months, and his mother lives with them. No wonder there are no babies. So when the woman left—a horrible woman—I called the daughter-in-law and asked her to come see me. 'But I don't even know you,' she said. 'That's not important,' I told her. Your mother-in-law came to see me.'

"Well, the poor thing came and she was crying like this (demonstrated) and I told her that once her mother-in-law was gone, everything would be fine. And then I saw the son and told him, 'Listen here, you've got to get rid of your mother. She can't live with you and your young wife.' And he said, 'I can't do that. She's all alone. When my father died I promised I'd look after her.' I told him that was nonsense. Anyway, finally the mother moved out and now the girl is expecting in two months. You know, she wasn't a pretty girl—just a nice girl."

Madame Langmann is writing an astrological book on Henry having to do with the age of Uranus. Like all the Europeans who come here, she commented on "our freedom." All the Europeans say the same thing.

"You have so much freedom. It's wonderful. In Switzerland there is no freedom—John Calvin was a terrible man. Switzerland is dominated by his thinking."

Of course we—having the wide-open freedom that is matched to the size of the country—appreciate it, or not. Is everything always a matter of contrasts? I do think so. Things in relationship to one another, not independently. Faith has no meaning in and of itself. It is important only in contrast to an existence that would render us all medium gray and horizontal. But we Americans take our freedom too much for granted. We should appreciate it, value it more. We are like children—all of us—squandering our resources blindly, heedlessly, as if there were a limitless supply.

I left with another Miller lithograph, a gorgeous one quite unlike anything else that I have or have seen of his. A pair of reclining lovers in intense blues and fuchsia tones. Very Picassoesque of the satyr period.

Henry was in a giving mood and also gave me a copy of *Joey* in which he wrote on the first page: "For Barbara, with all my heart." I nearly wept when I saw that for he is not given to emotional displays or excesses—except, of course, in the case of Brenda.

Joey is the third volume of his *Book of Friends* series but in this case is exclusively devoted to one friend, Alfred Perlès.

"I call it 'Joey' because we called each other Joey. 'Joey,' I'd say, and he would answer, 'Yes, Joey.' Joey is one of those adorable names. Do you notice that there are certain names that strike a chord in you? You react when you hear them."

"He wrote a wonderful book about you."

"Oh, yes, compared to that terrible book by Jay Martin. That horrible biography I never authorized! And which I tried to prevent him from doing. The one by Alfred Perlès is *My Friend, Henry Miller*, and it is a book of real love and simplicity."

"He gives a total picture of you as I recall."

"Oh yes. He knew my faults and in my book I remind him about how he would often correct me. He was quite a scholar. I must tell you, although this might not be appropriate. He was an Austrian in World War I, you see, and he was on the wrong side of the fence. Anyhow, he was of a good, bourgeois family and he was made a lieutenant without any knowledge of warfare at all. No military training. And he was a very sensitive man. He was a poet already then. And a great lover of Goethe, I want to tell you.

"So anyhow, he's on the front line and the order has been given, 'Don't give the order to fire until you see the whites of the enemy's eyes.' Now he watched the enemy approaching and as they got closer, he could see the whites of their eyes and he became paralyzed. He couldn't open his mouth. And fortunately a sergeant took over and gave the order or they'd have all been wiped out.

"But he was ordered to be executed. And his family, with the influence that it had, managed to have him committed to the insane asylum. So he spent the whole four years of the war in the insane asylum. And he read his head off. He read the most wonderful things. He discussed things with the other supposedly insane people."

"A lot of people have benefitted from asylums and prisons," I added. "The Marquis de Sade and Henry Cowell and Genet."

"There's one little sequel to that," Henry went on. "When he left the asylum he headed for Paris. And he knew French, he had had a French nurse as a child and he read French so he went to Paris and he lived in a little hotel, but he didn't know a soul and it was very hard for him being an Austrian, you know, to get acquainted and make friends with any Frenchmen. So in his loneliness he would write himself letters, post them and wait for them to come. He'd go down to the mailbox eagerly to see if 'my letter is there.' How do you like that?"

I told him I thought it was inspired and then asked him if Perlès and Anaïs had gotten on.

"No, that is something that comes out in my book on him. Anaïs treated all of us, except me because I was her lover, but Durrell, Perlès, Moricand, very cavalierly. You were either in her graces or out.

"And Joey, my friend Joey, he adored her. But he wrote about her in *My Friend Henry Miller* and told the truth about her. About her marriage and everything and that she was this and that. He was really trying to glorify her, and she was horrified by the truth. She didn't want anyone to know she had a husband then.

"So what does he do but he says, 'Alright, I'll write another book. So he makes another book in which he splits her in half. There are two women. One side of her is a dancer and the other is a writer and that only infuriated her more. And she wiped him out. She said, 'I don't want anything more to do with him.' And Durrell and I fought with her to reinstate him, but no, she wouldn't listen. She said he was a traitor."

"She'd probably laugh about that today, don't you think?"

"Oh, yes. She'd laugh about it now. But at that period it was very important for her to keep the lie going."

"One of the things that I love in your work is the correspondence with Anaïs, the hundreds of letters you wrote to her. When I asked her about her letters to you, she said, "Well, you know Henry. He couldn't be bothered to keep them."

"That's what she said...hmmm. I think they're probably in the UCLA Research Library."

November 8, 1979: Over dinner this evening Henry and I discussed the interview I'll be doing with him next week. His attention is completely focused on it so obviously he is looking forward to it. The interview will be aired over KCRW, December 26th on his 88th birthday. He has nothing else going on at the moment so he's worked himself up about this. I get letters from him with suggestions, calls from Bill Pickerill as well. It's really incredible. One would think that he would just sit back and rest on his well-earned laurels.

While he has never spoken about it, I think he feels terribly neglected by this country's lack of recognition of him. After all, he's never been publicly honored in any way in the United States, unless one counts the obscenity trials in the '60s as recognition, while in Europe he is revered as a poet and his name is empowered as if with magic. Because of his rage about America he has backed himself into a corner in a way. He's turned his back and thumbed his nose at the very institutions he now wishes would recognize him with awards and accolades. And even if they did honor and recognize him, he would still be against them. Even if he spits on them, however, they should still give him his due. He wants recognition, but on his terms.

My notes for the NPR interview: Ask him about his cooks, that living and doing art work are one and the same thing, "to beg as a saint is totally different than begging as an artist—the latter degrades you to the core of your being." Ask him to speak of his days of begging and poverty, of what he calls "his joyous misery"...

Insomnia—a book that turned all his misery over his fifth wife, Hoki Tokuda, into humor, joy. "Without love one is hopeless. Love is the spiritual food that we subsist on... Whenever I was in love I submitted totally. Complete submission, that's the thing... It's only now that I've learned to love a woman." Sex and Love. Eros and Agape—love between mortals versus love of God. Henry sees them as comingled.

"What we want in art is how it could be or might be—glorification. All exaggeration in art is for the best—life is too bleak—unless you're a joyous person—then you're dancing, but not every day."

Duality, spirituality, cosmic astrology...women, Cendrars, art and literature, D. H. Lawrence.

Miller's art, his work, is a mixture of the high and the low and an acceptance of the whole, of the totality of things. "If you look back in history you see that mankind in general has not been affected; mankind in general remains the scum of the earth."

One of his favorite words is "de-evolution," meaning that "We came down from angels to a mortal state. I don't think we started out as worms...the earth has room for everything. Acceptance—accept yourself. I never had any trouble with that."

November 16, 1979: I had dinner again tonight with Henry and Madame Langmann.

"Whenever I want to get around my husband, you know, or ask him something that he doesn't want to do, or ask him for something he doesn't think we need, you see, I make it just so," Madame Langmann told us. "Very agreeable, very nice. I wait until the evening and then I tell him that even though we've been married for 37 years, tonight is a night for a romantic dinner. And I serve him caviar and champagne. Just like that. And I make everything agreeable, very, very, agreeable."

"Caviar! Henry exclaimed. "But that's very expensive, isn't it?"

"Yes, but I have a good supply of it," Madame Langmann responded. "Whenever anyone asks me what they can get me, what do I want as a gift, I tell them to get me caviar or champagne. And so I have lots of caviar and lots of champagne."

I liked her immensely and her thinking as well. She's still a coquette and charming and rather quaint; from another age and another way of thinking. An original! She has invited Henry's entourage to visit her...Bill, Charles, myself and Brenda...

Henry hated *The Dream Tunnel*, a piece commissioned by the Los Angeles Philharmonic Orchestra for a series of Bicentennial Children's Concerts at the Music Center in Los Angeles; The premier performances were May 12, 13, 14, 1976. My husband and I had collaborated on the work; he wrote the music, I the libretto. And I ended up performing the piece as well for several of the performances.

However, he very much liked the first few pages of my book on Anaïs. "You've got it. You're on to it. Keep it simple like this... I think you knew her better than I."

"Not better, Henry. I knew her at a different time in her life. I knew a different woman."

Henry is shaky these days. He has been having dizzy spells and last week took a bad fall. I helped him to his bedroom tonight just to make sure he didn't have another accident.

Speaking with Henry about Anaïs, he said all the diary writing prevented her from living. That her minute analysis was constipating. "We must live, make mistakes and live with those mistakes. They are a part of us." I told him that I thought the diary was Anaïs's *Wild Duck* (the Ibsen play about the moral dilemma between a militant idealism and his own worldly temperament) and that the diary can be an abdication of responsibility for oneself in relationship to the world.

November 23, 1979: Henry on Brenda: "She keeps me alive. Without her I wouldn't be able to go on."

He is so very tired these days. His eyes are bothering him; his hearing is deteriorating as well. The torture of old age.

He wrote a letter to the Guggenheim telling them I should get a grant. "I told them I was writing with such fervor because I never got one."

On November 30, 1979 I wrote Henry:

> Dear Henry,
>
> Last night I forgot to tell you about the radio interviews we did. NPR (National Public Radio) is editing them as follows: They're excerpting your voice and comments and mixing those segments with an actor reading from your work. (I presume they will cut me out entirely, which is understandable, I suppose.) They plan to air the program on your birthday, December 26. These particular tapes went directly to Washington as I told you. After they finish producing the program they'll offer it to all their stations throughout the country. Ruth has already scheduled it for KCRW, her station in Santa Monica. I can't imagine how I forgot to mention it to you. My mind must have been on something else.

Henry's response was written December 4, 1979:

> Dear Barbara,
>
> Was surprised to get your letter about N.P.R. today. Do you want me to write them (where exactly) and say I don't want it done their way—what I did is with you and not an actor.
>
> I don't give a damn about birthday celebrations. I think it's an insult to you! (How did your good friend Ruth let this happen?).

Henry Miller: The Last Days

They sure aren't doing me a favor. Perhaps they think they are.
Cheers!
Henry

After receiving Henry's letter I phoned NPR and spoke to the woman who was producing the program; the conversation barely lasted two minutes.

Jo Ellen: "We have a problem? Miller is unhappy with the idea of an actor spliced in between his dialogue? Well, what does he want?"

Me: "He wants the interview to run just as it was recorded, with me as the interviewer."

Jo Ellen: "Well, I'll have to send you back the tapes."

Me: "You don't want to run it as a straight interview?"

Jo Ellen: "Sure, we want it. But I can't have Henry Miller dictating to me. We do a lot of interviews and no one tells us how to use the material."

Me: "Well, he *is* Henry Miller. But fine, send them back then."

I hung up and was writing about the above conversation and my disappointment when the phone rang and it was NPR. "We'll do it the way you recorded it."

December 9, 1979: The other night Henry related a marvelous story about one of his great loves, a German woman named Renate whom he says I resemble with my hair cut short as it is now.

"She wrote to me recently and told me that she had been quite ill. The doctors recommended surgery, which she refused. Instead she went off to Greece to cure herself. She rented a house on a small island and she recovered. She liked it so much there that she decided to buy the house in which she was staying. Like Durrell, she's decided to spend half the year in Germany and the other half in Greece in the sun. And the man she bought the house from sold it to her to get the money for an operation that he needed."

Apparently Henry is adding to and making changes in his will. He told me that he had added a conduit leaving all his clothes to Bill. Marvelous that. Only someone who has been really hard up knows what that means and would think of such a thing. Henry's word of the week: Apocatastasis—the eternal round. The planets make their rounds. His planet's journey is nearly complete, entering the cycle where it was when he was born.

December 10, 1979: KCRW press release:

KCRW SALUTES HENRY MILLER

The legendary American writer Henry Miller celebrates his 88th year on Wednesday, December 26. In observance of this birthday, KCRW (89.9) presents *Conversation with Henry Miller* at 11:00 a.m. and again at 9:30 p.m.

The program, an interview conducted by writer Barbara Kraft at Miller's Pacific Palisades home, presents an intimate and informal hour of talk and recollection. Miller remembers his "joyous misery," the Paris years he worked on the seminal *Tropics*. He comments on love and sex, spirituality and cosmic astrology. He advocates art as glorification.

KCRW will program that day's morning concert (9-11 a.m.) as a birthday tribute to Miller, playing his favorite artists, composers and recordings.

The writer, who is a local resident, is expected to tune in to KCRW for this special celebration.

December 18, 1979: Music that Henry chose for his birthday concert included:

Maurice Ravel's *Gaspard de la Nuit*, anything sung by John McCormick, *The Rose of Picardy* sung by Thomas Burke, Cantor Sirota singing *R'zei*, which was one of his favorites. Sirota had a dramatic coloratura tenor voice and was often called the "Jewish Caruso." The list continued with "anything by Amato and Caruso," the *Liebestod* from *Tristan and Isolde*, *Suwannee River*, *My Old Kentucky Home*, Scriabin's *Fifth Sonata*, Fats Waller singing *Two Sleepy People* and *Meet Me in Dreamland*.

December 23, 1979: Over dinner last night Henry gave me an "injection," to use his word. An infusion. He said that he's been terribly depressed of late and told me that he is "nearly suicidal."

When I was telling him about Arne's daughter and how she died of an overdose, he responded, "I wish I knew what one could take like that and just not wake up. When I'm like this I think it must have something to do with the planets. Have you seen the moon? Don't you think it's connected with that?"

Brenda is still in Mississippi, hence his depression. She is vital to his well-being and sense of himself. He needs to be in love and to have someone love him too. It's always been the juice of his life. Even if it is all fantasy.

And then on a different subject: "Barbara, I have no doubt about you. You're a born writer. People like you and me, we make our whole life literature. The rest of the world doesn't understand, but for people like us that is all there is. Now, Anaïs didn't have this love of literature. She didn't have the passion of the great artist. She lacked passion. She talked a lot about how she read, but her reading was spotty and unorganized."

He was right about Anaïs. I had never thought of it before, but a passion, at least for literature, was indeed missing. She didn't love books like Henry and I do. Whereas Henry and I talk books and literature all the time, I never had similar conversations with Anaïs.

And that is why her relationship with Rupert worked so well. He was not an intellectual, nor was she. He was a very handsome, physical man, a simple man despite the fact that he had been brought up in a sophisticated worldly world. His father was the English actor Reginald Pole and his stepfather was Lloyd Wright, the son of Frank Lloyd Wright. Interestingly, Rupert attended Harvard University at the same time as John F. Kennedy.

Sixteen years younger than she, he loved the outdoors, and when he and Anaïs came to California he earned a living as a forest ranger. Despite all her lies and subterfuge, both Rupert and Hugo loved her and adored her and cared for her. For them Anaïs could do no wrong. For both men she was an inspiration, like one of the mythological Greek muses who personified knowledge and the arts, especially literature and the arts.

There was a transcendent aura that seemed to hover over her like an invisible halo. And indeed she was a special creature.

Henry Miller: The Last Days

I told Henry that I was having trouble writing the book about her. "You know, if I did it as fiction, I would have so much more freedom. And I'm afraid of telling the truth again. I paid such a high price the last time around."

"Truth is everything, Barbara. Tell them the truth. Truth is a wonderful thing, and this is from a man who can tell some tall lies. Yet at the same time truth embraces everything and it's worth it. I can't tell you what it means to me to get letters from all over the world about just that—that I told the truth. No, you go to it and write in all the things you've told me about. It will make it stronger, better.

"Write books, though. Make everything a book. Your apprenticeship is over. No more short pieces. No one wants them nowadays. You can't sell them."

And so I will—the ambivalences, the doubt, the anger and the love.

Henry on Blaise Cendrars: "There's a renewed interest in Cendrars these days. They have a Cendrars organization in Laguna Beach and they wrote to me and made me an honorary member. He was a man of action. He did everything. He once asked me if I liked Proust and I said, 'Yes, I do,' and he was surprised. He said that Proust looked back. And I said, 'Yes, that's what was so good about it.' He didn't understand my love for Lawrence either.

"One of Cendrar's books ends with the word 'mystery.' He writes about how an arm fell from the sky, cut off above the elbow, you know. It fell from the sky and dropped to the ground. The hand stuck in the earth and the rest of the arm stuck up in the air with the blood gushing out still. He ends this with the word mystery."

"It makes me think of Knut Hamsun," Henry continued. "He told the Norwegians they should be like the Germans and they hated him for that. He was accused of being a collaborator. But he went to the Germans and tried to talk them into being easier on the Norwegians. But Hitler wouldn't listen to him. Hamsun never told this story to anyone."

"I was in Norway once, Henry. It has such a provincial feeling to it. An idea can't breathe in Oslo. That's the feeling you get. Ibsen hated the smugness and complacency of the Norwegians, as did Munch. They both wrote and painted about this deadly hothouse existence, which didn't seem so different during the couple of weeks that I was there. The same still, tidy going about one's affairs. At the same time they have the highest drug rate per capita in the world. And Sweden the highest suicide rate. Or at least it did the last time I checked. That said, the most intense love affair I ever had was with a Norwegian composer."

We talked about Iran then and Henry observed that Khomeini was a religious fanatic stirring up a holy war. "The man's crazy. Not to them and their way of thinking. But he is crazy."

People are constantly writing to Henry asking for money and he usually complies.

"I got a letter from a man who called himself Mikelas asking me for money the other day," Henry said. "Could I help him? I wrote back and said, 'Sure, but what's your real name?' I had the feeling he was of Polish or Russian descent. He was of both. I wrote him and told him I'd send him a check for a $100 or $200 if he'd just tell me how to make it out, what name to put on it."

Henry Miller: The Last Days

And to me about my writing... "That device you have of speaking to a person as if they were still alive and here, that's wonderful. So effective. Why don't you write to *The New Republic* or any of the magazines and see if they'd pay you to write a review of *Joey*. You like *Joey*, don't you?"

While I loved and love *The New Republic* and have subscribed to it for years, neither Henry nor I would ever find a place in its august pages.

That last year of his life, Henry shuffled between his old-fashioned, high-set, walnut-dark bed, the desk at its foot, the Ping-Pong table in the lanai where he painted, a more sedentary kind of play for an octogenarian, and the redwood picnic table covered with a checked cloth where he held court every evening attired in his bathrobe, plaid or blue terrycloth, pajamas, bedroom slippers and white socks.

He was a tough old bird, rather like a turkey, with his croaky voice, heavily veined, creped hands, parchment-thin skin, wattled throat and indomitable, naked head.

His real and lasting passion was for his work. He was also a man who liked himself and venerated life. Why else marry five times and father three children? He believed that art was glorification and that paradise was a creation of the individual mind, available to anyone, anywhere, regardless of the circumstances in which they found themselves.

"I keep my nose to the grindstone," he said one night over dinner. "Old age is terrible. It's a disease of the joints. It's awful when I get up in the morning. I can barely bend over to brush my teeth. It's only when I get to work solving problems that I forget about it."

Beset by a multitude of infirmities the last decade of his life, Miller worked as furiously as ever producing several books and hundreds of watercolors. He continued to maintain his voluminous correspondence with the world and entertained visitors, ranging from immigrants to celebrities.

As his body failed him, the eyes, the ears, the bowels, the bladder, the bones, he shrugged his shoulders and with head held high said, "We must accept what comes, don't you know?"

And then he would return to the arduous business of folding the napkin in front of him. The long-fingered, still graceful hands slowly smoothing the cloth, folding it in half, in quarters. This accomplished, he would labor to roll the napkin up, fitting it, at length and with considerable effort, into the monogrammed silver napkin holder that marked his place at table. One tiny island of control that could still be mastered with great concentration.

Though Henry accepted what was happening to him, there were moments when he flapped his wings in annoyance, an appropriate response for a man who had steadfastly refused to be overcome by anything.

His humble efforts to carry on with his life were at times moving, at times exhausting, at times hysterically funny and at all times immensely and universally human. For Miller was not and never desired to be "somebody" in the sense that today everybody is somebody, either through earned or unearned celebrity or through some vicarious attachment to celebrity. He was a man who would rather be at peace with himself than a writer, according to his friend, Wallace Fowlie. Although, with all due respect to Mr. Fowlie, Miller's rapprochement with peace was achieved by writing, which ordered and transformed the Milleresque chaos into a turbulent and teeming celebration of life on his terms.

On this particular Friday evening, some six months before he died, I had to awaken him to come to the table. Usually he was up waiting for me, but of late he had become so weak that he was no longer able to navigate alone the distance between bedroom and dining room. He suffered from some kind of palsy, possibly caused by petit mal seizures, and was quite frail. His hands trembled, he was paralyzed on one side, deaf in one ear and blind in one eye, so he said, although he regularly commented on what I was wearing down to a pair of green suede cowboy boots I once showed up in. When sight failed him, his sense of smell came to the fore. "I can smell your perfume, Barbara. Hmmmmm. I can barely see anymore but I can still smell." The full lips gathered into a lopsided grin, exposing teeth that remained remarkably virile.

I roused the slight body that was all but invisible under the satin-covered down comforter and eased him into the waiting walker. At dinner that night he spoke about how he would come back as "a man who tends flowers. Not a genius, or a writer, that's the worst... People used to envy me my inspiration. I hate inspiration. It takes you over completely."

But he never did get rid of "it"—of inspiration. Nor did he rid himself of his obsession with woman, with

Eros, with life itself. Woman, Eros and life were vital to Miller's sense of himself, imbued with a mystery and a magic that compelled and obsessed and bemused him without letup until June 7, 1980—the day his eternal round was completed.

January 1980: I dreamt last night that I was helping an old, old man to die. In the dream, it was someone who looked like Igor Stravinsky whom I was fortunate to meet once. For the old man in the dream the dying was prolonged, hard and tiring.

Like Henry at the table now, his head drooping, his thoughts uncompleted, dropping off mid-sentence, his coffee-flavored ice cream melting slowly between shaky spoonfuls. There is a little dish of vitamins and supplements to his right, which he takes after dinner, swallowing them down with his coffee. I have rarely seen him dressed in anything other than his pajamas and bathrobe, but he is always so clean. Charles takes such good care of him, bathing and shaving him every morning and helping him into a fresh pair of pajamas.

January 10, 1980: Over dinner Monday evening, Henry told me, "Bill and I have been trying to figure out your flaws, what they are. We can't find any. But you have so much trouble. Perhaps you should have your horoscope done to see what's going on. Maybe it will tell you something."

Brenda is back from wherever she was off to and Henry rose to the occasion full of energy and vitality. He is painting again—several watercolors a day. Amazing. Two weeks ago I thought he wasn't long for this world.

He, too, felt he might not make it. L'amour. Even if she is an opportunist, it's on such a small scale, one can only be amused and mildly put off by it. And there is something charming about her relationship with Henry. It is touching despite what Noel Young told me about her last night.

Apparently she was not in the original version of *Joey* that Henry sent to him at Capra. "She drove up to Santa Barbara to have lunch with me and asked me how come Henry hadn't written a chapter on her. She worked on me to work on Henry, and I did. I wrote to him and suggested that he add a chapter on Brenda and that's how it came about."

January 19, 1980: At dinner last night it was obvious that Henry is failing. I think the end is near. He is beginning to enter a final decline, although he struggles mightily to hold on to the reality of life outside his fumbling body. But still he sinks more and more into the abyss of the self, dropping off during dinner mid-sentence, returning eventually to the company at the table but no longer able to pick up the next word and continue on as if nothing had happened.

His hand shook so when he picked up the saltshaker that I had to rescue it from him and salt his food for him. It's so sad, so hard to see. I do love that old man. He has given so much to me, to the world. His life has mattered; he has made a difference in the order of things. Yet a part of me wants to turn my back on him because I'm tired of death, of sitting with death, of holding death in my arms. I don't want to suffer another loss. When he goes, I'll really be on my own. I dread the loss of another "surrogate parent"—first Anaïs and now Henry.

Before I left last night I went to his bedroom to make certain he was comfortable. He was at his desk writing and looked up as I stood in the doorway.

"Oh, Barbara, you're still here. Would you mind cutting my fingernails for me? S hasn't had time to do it for a while now and they're beginning to curl over and crack...be careful you don't cut me."

January 26, 1980: Ruth went with me last night to Henry's for dinner. I need someone to go along now as I cannot manage cooking, taking care of him and conversing with him at the same time. He continues to weaken, is frailer each time I see him. He seems to be literally wasting away; the doctors say he is suffering from both malnutrition and protein deficiency.

He no longer comes to the table by himself. At 7 p.m. I went to tell him dinner was ready and found him asleep, mouth agape, head arched back as if he were struggling to claim the air. It is heart-rending seeing him like that. He is no longer *the* Henry Miller, but a mere mortal reduced and humbled and yearning for release as we will all one day yearn for release.

I woke him and asked if he needed my help.

"No, I can manage by myself."

I started to leave the room and then turned back to make certain he was okay. He was struggling to raise himself up and got only as far as supporting himself on his elbows. There he stayed while a spasm ran through his emaciated body like an electric current. He dropped back to the pillow, exhausted. I went to help him and pulled him up gently, he holding tight to my hands.

"Henry," I said, "It's like Ed Hokum told you last week, 'this is your mountain now.'"

Ruth's presence stimulated him and they carried on together as he and I once did. But I'm family now and can no longer play the role of scintillating guest bringing the world with me to the dinner table. While they talked, I got dinner on the table and tended to his specific needs. He rallied in Ruth's presence and talked like the Henry of old. It's still the best conversation in town, the mind remarkably untouched by age and its incumbent infirmities given the right stimulation.

They spoke of Paris, literature in general, and French literature, that of Lautréamont—the self-styled Comte de Lautréamont who wrote *Les Chants de Maldoror*, an early surrealist work devoted to the principle of evil, the religion of evil.

Ruth told us that her ex-husband referred to Lautrémont as the "Count No-Count." Henry and she spoke of the café life, of the French toilets, of Hermann Hesse and Thomas Mann. Henry's favorite Hesse book is *Siddheartha*, which is arguably Hesse's signature book.

"*The Glass Bead Game* was too much for me," he said. "It went over my head."

"I struggled through it, too," Ruth responded. "But when I got to the end, it was worth it. The whole book is the ending. The old argument between Dionysius and Apollo."

Henry told us of being in Germany and seeing huge bowls in the restrooms. "I asked what are they for—for washing clothes?—and I was told they were for vomiting.

The Germans drink so much, you know. And so they'd come in and vomit. Pigs."

He again spoke of how he would come back an ordinary man—"I think it so wonderful in *Siddhartha* when Hesse has Christ come back just an ordinary man."

"Well, Einstein said he wanted to come back as a plumber," Ruth commented. "Why is that, Henry? Some people yearn to be possessed, by anything, and never are. And yet you are, were possessed. Is it a curse or a blessing?"

"It's a curse," Henry responded. "Yes, it's like a flame. It owns you. It has possession over you. You are not master of yourself. You are consumed by this thing. And the books you write. They're not you. They're not me sitting here, this Henry Miller. They belong to someone else. It's terrible. You can never rest."

And so it went—the café life, the honor and esteem given to the poets and writers by the French.

"You know, on the passport where you have to put down your occupation, I put down *écrivain* and the man looked at me and said, 'Écrivain...hmmmm...come have a drink with me,' and so we went to the nearest café and we had a drink together. It was wonderful. To be a poet, a writer, is a wonderful thing in France. You're treated as a serious man, with respect and dignity.

"Now, when I went to England once, it was a different story. I went to England to have a vacation, don't you know... And when the ship docked and I went with my passport to the customs officer, he asked, 'You're a writer?' And I said, 'Yes, I am,' and he said, 'What have you written?' and I mentioned the *Tropic* books, and he got out a big book and looked them up and said, 'They're not in here. Are you sure they're not medical books?' Then he asked me how much money I had with me and I had about the equivalent of two or three dollars. And he said, 'Were you planning to have a vacation on that?' And I said, 'Oh, no. I'm to meet a friend who's bringing me some money.'

"Anyway, he said they'd put me up in a cell for the night and send me back to France the next day. And so that's where I spent the night—in jail, in a cell. And when I had to go to the toilet, they wouldn't even let me close the door. Can you imagine that? The next morning they put me back on the boat for Dieppe, which is where I met the man who took me for a drink in a café because I was a writer, a poet."

"That's the English for you," Ruth responded. "Even today if you mention William Blake to someone they'll say, 'Oh yes, the painter.' They don't know anything about his being a great writer."

Last night she told a charming story about going to one of the cemeteries in Paris, one of the smaller ones. It seems she was stopped from entering because she was wearing a sleeveless blouse. She said to the guard, "But how can you do that when you have Baudelaire buried here?"

Henry stayed at the table a very long time for these days. He did not drop off once and the conversation was vibrant and enthusiastic as of old. I helped him to bed then and as I turned out the light he said, "Barbara, thank you for a wonderful night."

He's given so much to the world, to life; it would seem somehow that his dying might be eased, that the passage would occur through the simple corridor of sleep.

I'm so busy trying to be safe these days it's ridiculous—whatever "safe" means. As Faulkner writes so pointedly in *As I Lay Dying*, safe isn't necessarily good:

> When something is new and hard and bright, there ought to be something a little better for it than just being safe, since the safe things are just the things that folks have been doing so long they have worn the edges off and there's nothing to the doing of them that leaves a man to say, That was not done before and it cannot be done again.

Passion is one kind of truth, art another. Are there any others?

January 27, 1980: Henry is so terribly fragile now. I am almost afraid to touch or embrace him for fear he will break. Bird-like. His eyes once darkly intent and focused outward retreat now from the world into a bird's nest of dried twigs and tired bones.

The doctors say that he is suffering from malnutrition. No one is in the house to prepare breakfast or lunch for him. S controls everything; all the checks and related business go through her. Someone told me that her mother is Henry's accountant as well as his lawyer. I have no idea if that is true or not. What I do know is that he is alone in that house with only her friends who live upstairs to care for him and they could not care less. They are all heavy dopers—as is she, drinkers and derelicts.

I took things into my own hands and went to see her today. I phoned and phoned to no avail, so I found out where she was living now and drove over to see her.

It was 4:30 on a Sunday afternoon. Her car was parked in the driveway, one tire very nearly flat. The morning newspaper was on the doorstep, wrapped in plastic against the gray threat of the day. Heaviness hung in the air, matching my mood. A light sprinkle began as I walked up to the house and rang the doorbell.

I rang the bell repeatedly but no one answered though I sensed there were people inside. I wrote a note I intended to leave when I heard a sound as if someone were stumbling about inside. So I rang the bell again. Instinct only kept me on that uninviting doorstep. A thick, male voice finally penetrated through the locked door. "Who's there?"

"It's Barbara Kraft and I've come to see S."

"Well, she's asleep now."

"Well, it is very important that I see her now. So get her up."

A long pause… "Okay."

Several minutes passed and then a whining, thin, petulant female voice came through the shut door. "What is it?"

"It's Barbara Kraft, S, and I need to speak to you."

The door opened slowly. Once a pretty woman, S was now ravaged and worn, ravaged by the constant use of drugs and the men who come and go and support the drugs and use her along with the drugs. She stood in the dark doorway, tying a maroon colored robe around her emaciated body. Her tawny thick hair, the one beauty left to her, luxuriantly tumbling into a mass around her wasted face.

"Is something wrong? Should I get dressed and go to the house?"

"No. I've come to talk to you. I've tried to reach you for days but could not get through."

"I had my number changed because so many people are bothering me."

"Well, I'd like to talk with you."

"Now? But it's Sunday. That's why I had my phone changed."

"This is important." I was still on the doorstep. It was difficult to find her eyes behind the screen door that separated us. "I'd like to come in and speak with you and it won't wait. Unless you'd rather come out and sit in the car and talk."

"My house is a mess."

"I don't care about your house."

She finally opened the screen door, not because she wanted to but because I gave her no other choice. It had to be obvious to her that I had no intention of leaving.

"I've come to speak to you about Henry. I've never meddled in your affairs or become involved in all the intrigues and arguments that go on in that house. But now I must because things have gone too far. Henry is alone all the time and he's failing rapidly and he needs someone in the house to take care of him."

And so it went. She was on the defensive, evasive, manipulative and shrewd. "But Barry and Linda are there..." (Barry and Linda were friends of hers who were billeted in the upstairs bedrooms free of rent when she moved out.)

"It's not good enough, S. I'm not criticizing them or you. I'm simply saying there must be someone else whose main concern is Henry."

"Well, I'm here and they can always call me. I'm only five minutes away."

"No one can reach you, S. Not even Henry. And as you just said a minute ago, you had your phone number changed. So how can he reach you? Now, I know that everyone's been down on you, attacking you. I know what goes on and I can tell you that when the shit hits the fan you're going to be the one who gets it. Because you're in charge and being paid to take care of Henry and Henry doesn't have proper care. You're not even there."

I suggested then that Bill Pickerill move in the house. A suggestion she avoided, saying, "But Henry doesn't want Bill there."

That took me completely by surprise. "What do you mean, he doesn't want Bill there?"

"It's come up before and each time Henry has said that Bill makes him nervous and he doesn't want him living there."

"S, I find that very hard to believe. Henry's very fond of Bill and is always disappointed when Bill's not there for dinner."

"I know, but still, he doesn't want him to live there."

I knew she was lying but could hardly accuse her of lying as it would have done no good in any event. So I shifted ground. "I still think you should consider speaking to Henry about Bill moving in. You know, if what's going on in that house got out, it would not look very good. In fact, it would look very tacky."

"What do you mean? That people come home late once in a while and a little drunk?"

"I'm just saying it would be a real scandal, a public scandal, and you will be held responsible if something dreadful should happen. I mean, how would you feel if Henry were to die all alone? Can you imagine how the kids would turn on you? If you had Bill there the pressure would be off of you as well as some of the responsibility. And if Bill were there, he couldn't criticize and shake his finger at you like he does now."

We walked to the door and she said she would have to give some thought to what I had said. I saw that if it was possible she would let the whole thing ride, so I turned and looked straight at her and said: "I don't mean this to be a threat, but I should tell you that if something isn't done to rectify the situation in that house, I'll write about the whole thing, and, believe me, it wouldn't look too pretty on the page and in print... I don't mean to threaten you but..."

I left then and stopped for a drink with Bill Pickerill. On my way home, I drove by Henry's house, out of instinct and because I had the feeling that S had probably dashed over there as fast as possible to sit at Henry's bedside and fill him with a lot false information. I felt as if I were in the midst of a B-plot in a second-rate movie.

I went home and waited for her to call with her decision. When she didn't phone I realized I would have to go directly to Henry and immediately. So the next morning, Monday, I picked up the key to the house from Bill and went over around noon. It was unlikely that S would stagger in before 1 p.m.

Henry Miller: The Last Days

When I arrived Charles was getting ready to leave; he'd finished bathing and shaving Henry and had just put him back into his bed. He let me in somewhat reluctantly, but I assured him it was the right thing to do. I went into Henry's bedroom and woke him up. Henry was surprised to see me and somewhat befuddled by my presence. Propping pillows behind his back, I helped him to sit up and stuck his hearing aids into his ears.

I sat down on the bed next to him and took his hand in mine. "Henry, I've come to talk to you. You know, I'm very worried about you."

"I know you are, Barbara. S was here last night and told me you were concerned. But I'm all right, you know. There're people around. Linda and Barry upstairs. He's a good guy. He's trying to write a book, you know."

I very much doubted the book business but said nothing.

"Henry, what I came to talk about is Bill Pickerill. Did S tell you about him?"

"About Bill? No. What about Bill?"

"Well, Bill has to leave Gordy Hormel's place. He's been fired, let go, although I didn't tell S that. I just told her he was ready to leave and had no place to go. I asked her to speak to you about his moving in here and she told me that you didn't want him here. I found that hard to believe."

"Did she say that? I'm amazed. I've always told Bill he'd have a place with me if he ever needed it. Why didn't he come to talk to me?"

"He was afraid to, Henry. And then S makes him feel unwelcome, and she told me you didn't want him here because he made you nervous."

"She said that?"

"Yes. Henry, she lies to you all the time. I know that Val and Tony have tried to talk to you about her."

"They wanted me to get rid of her but they never told me why."

"They wanted you to get rid of her because she's a drug addict."

"Oh, you know about that?"

"Yes. But it's not just a little problem. The first time I brought Harry here to the house to meet you he asked me what S was on. You remember him, don't you? He told you how he was the first Jew ever in the FBI and that he worked in drugs. He said it looked like S was either on heroin or speed. You know, her body is completely wasted, skeletal. She looks terrible and is in no shape to take care of anyone. She can't even take care of herself, let alone anyone else."

"But she's a good secretary. She's very bright and inside I think she's a good woman."

"Yes, Henry, I agree. I just think since Bill needs a home it would be good for everyone concerned if he could stay here for a while."

"Yes, of course he can stay here. Let me see, I think he told me there were four bedrooms upstairs."

"I think there are only three, Henry, but maybe Barry could go…"

"No, I couldn't do that. Let's see, there's Barry's room and Linda's and then there's a third bedroom that I keep free for Val and I think there's a fourth bedroom. Anyway, tell Bill to come and see me."

It turned out that there were only three bedrooms upstairs and all three were occupied. Thus, Henry offered

Bill the couch in the living room. As Bill said, it took an act of God to get him into the house, to get someone responsible in situ, my word, not his. In fact, it took an act of "Barbara," and I'm enormously relieved that I was able to bring this off. I can leave with a clear conscience now, knowing that someone who genuinely cares about Henry is on board.

I hate to be overcome by anything. I refuse to be overcome.—Henry Miller

February 1980: Bill is in the process of moving into Henry's although he's not yet spent the night there. S came in and we made peace, at least on the surface. What she really feels is another issue. But she knows when she's been beaten and had the good sense to come in and make peace. She's trying to "tidy up the house" in the colloquial sense, which is all I wanted. I don't give a damn if she robs Henry blind (and I have no real evidence that she is other than for Bill's accusations and the fact that her habit is not a small one.)

Dinner was tedious because Henry is so weak. He ate a little and even commented on how good the food was. Then an attack of palsy forced him to push his plate away. His head drooping, he lapsed into one of those silent, ominous periods during which conversation stands still while we all wait in anticipation and tense hesitation for him to return to us. After a minute or two he came back slowly. "I'm sorry to be a bore."

He fights so hard, so hopelessly, so stubbornly and tenaciously to hold his own.

With all of this—the palsy, the lapses—the moment he comes up again he reaches for his glass and drinks down some of the enriched, high-caloric fluid that is now a stable of his new diet.

And he insists on pouring the remains from the can into the glass himself. Pushes any help away.

Bill kept trying to get him to leave the table and go to bed. But he wouldn't go until he was ready. He refuses to be told or be led. Good for him!

Like an old, fuzzy spider I feel him weaving a web around all of us. It's not yet his web, only a web. It's not yet done. There is still time to escape, back out, slip away. He had a difficult time sitting upright and kept listing to the left like a ship in a heavy wind. We all feared he would fall out of this chair and indeed would have had the chair been armless, which it wasn't.

"Am I leaning? I feel as if I'm going to fall."

And through it all he retains his dignity and an aura of control, and indeed it is Henry who still commands the situation.

No one dares help him until he is ready to allow them to do so. He doesn't tolerate help; he "allows" one to help him. One does not do it without his permission.

The struggle is noble, heroic, inspiring, all of which I told him. It is also sad, which I did not tell him.

"Henry, it's inspiring to watch you fight. I hope you don't mind but since you can't write about this, I am. In the diary."

"Oh no, I don't mind. That's fine, Barbara."

Henry Miller: The Last Days

February 5, 1980: A call from S asking me to speak to Henry about seeing his daughter Barbara after which I was going to call Barbara saying I'd speak to her father. But I changed my mind. It's not up to me to meddle in these old, worn-out affairs. Henry would quite rightly be alarmed and would no doubt see it as betrayal on my part. And indeed it would be. My loyalty is to him, not to an unknown woman of nearly 60 who was quite accidently the original liaison between her father and myself. In the end I changed my mind back again, called Barbara and was there for the meeting between the two of them; Henry is *her* father, not mine.

No wonder he's not close to her. She's whining and self-pitying and has nothing much to offer anyone. She told me that after five minutes or so she has nothing left to say to Henry because her interests are not his. She complained, "He's not interested in business, which is my life."

She still goes to see the therapist whom we briefly shared. Some five years now. "He's helped me tremendously. The things I've dealt with in that room about Henry." And yet, after five years, she still can't pick up a phone and call her father herself. I think she should change therapists or give up the process entirely.

February 8, 1980: One of the problems facing Henry is that his arteries are corroded and he's not getting enough oxygen to the brain. But still he fights on. The dignity of the man remains intact. He's remarkable and touching and funny. Hates going to the doctor, as do I.

As he said, "I hate to be taken over by anything."

Although he remains weakened and is generally failing, his spirits seem better now that Bill Pickerill is living in the house with him. I no longer have the sense of him moving away from us. The retreat into the final shell of the self has temporarily been halted. He perches on the abyss, more fish than goat now and the final dissolution is at hand. But he is not alone with it anymore. The stage is set for the last act, an act that could not begin until the house was put in order. And that is what Bill's presence has done. He has brought with him a sense of well-being, of integrity, of goodness.

Now that there was a semblance of order and regularity in the household, chaos gradually took up residence in Henry's innermost being—perhaps death knocking on his door felt like chaos to him.

He had always been an orderly man, and while he had lived a life of chaos and indeed preached the virtues of chaos, it was more of an abstraction than a reality. Of late, however, he had taken to scribbling the word across his more recent watercolors.

And still, given all that was going on inside of him, his watercolors, pens, papers remain arranged in an orderly fashion on the Ping-Pong table. He himself is always meticulously put together, albeit in pajamas, bathrobe and slippers, and he doesn't have the smell of an elderly person either...God bless Charles.

A house breathes the air of those who live in it. There is reciprocity between house and dweller, silent as the air is silent, yet a reality that permeates and touches all those who move within its walls. Prior to Bill's coming, a pall had spread over the house on Ocampo Drive. There was the upstairs and the downstairs, two unrelated parts, not even halves that did not match up or meet or fit together.

Nothing could grow or come to a fitting end in that deadly atmosphere. The only life lived was in the downstairs corner bedroom and there the wick burned low, fluttering and flickering, struggling to catch one more breath in the encroaching darkness. The upstairs people passed in and out, feeble witnesses to the end of a noble game. A game well fought, but a game whose end was imminent.

Please, God, do not let it end without someone in attendance, someone who will see and ease, someone to whom the passing will have meaning, someone who can use it, learn from it, record it, treasure it, write it all down and share it.

Bill has settled in the living room with his table and paints, his illuminated letters, his books and records and tapes. Enthusiasms that reflect his optimism. The room, formerly one in which the drapes were never opened, is now filled with the light and the energy of a young man. And his energy and vitality will hold back the darkness a while longer and Henry will not go into that dark night alone. The final crossing will be made holding hands with the hand of life. This I know. This I feel in my bones. The man who has given so much of himself to life will not go out without life around him. And that is how it should be and must be.

Henry told me that "art is glorification." To me the ultimate glorification is that art turns around and serves life. Lux Aeterna.

Henry's note to Bill written on the flyleaf of a new notebook that Bill asked Henry to "break in" for him:

> For Brother Bill Pickerill of the Order of the Cappadocian monks—a few words of compassion and nutriment to a fellow swimmer. This is your time, your place, your opportunity. Make the most of it; squeeze all the color out of the tubes. Dance the dance of seven veils. Make merry desperately. There only comes this one time. To us an eternity, to the gods, a passing shadow. Make believe your studio gives out on the Riviera. There really ain't any such place except in the mind. Have a good headache cum baccalaureate... Brother Henry, 2/7/80.

When Henry came out Friday night for dinner, he again commented appreciatively on my perfume. Bill has begun to help him more, even feeding him when necessary. Henry lets him do it. He is gradually letting go, allowing Bill to do more and more for him. It is very touching to watch these two men together—the rapport and affection between them. I wonder what Bill's father was or is like. Now as I write this, I realize that he has never mentioned anything about his personal life.

He is graceful and handles Henry with love and respect and tenderness, nearly like that of a woman. There is no intrusion on Henry's person. No violation to his dignity. And even as old and as infirm as he is, the room still comes alive when he enters it. Somehow he remains compelling; his presence powerful and dominant. Warm, observant, sometimes wicked, and on occasion still sage-like. He makes no demands and never complains. He observes and comments on his own condition with detachment—as if he were standing outside his body watching it falter. He is slightly quizzical, slightly surprised at his waning powers, but still in some sort of touch with what he once was.

February 11, 1980: Last night while I was speaking with Bill Pickerill on the phone, Henry wandered through the room. I could hear his voice in the distance, throaty from years of cigarettes and powerful. "Oh, Bill I see you're on the telephone. I didn't mean to disturb you." And with that he went back to his room, either to bed or to his desk. All night long he gets up and down.

But now, blessedly, he's no longer alone and can wander around, say hello to someone and go back to his own world, safe and secure. He can let go and allow his thoughts to dwell on what is ahead of him. He can prepare himself. My God, they were letting the man die of malnutrition and neglect and I stopped it. I called a halt to it, and it is because of my actions that Henry has Bill with him. Aggressiveness does have some virtues attached to it!

February 22, 1980: I haven't been able to get to Henry's for two weeks because of the torrential rain. Today was dry for the first time in nine days, but the roads were still littered with debris and high banks of mud.

Bill takes such good care of him, with utmost tenderness and warmth, and yet there is the distance of mutual respect between them. But Henry finally feels free to call on Bill to help him. Bill told me that Henry is up and down during the night and often takes a fall. Then he calls out, "Bill, are you there? I need some help."

Bill added, "There's all this arguing and bickering over who is going to get what. The other day S and Brenda got in a terrible row over the film rights to three of Henry's biggest works. He had told Brenda that he'd give them to her and then S found out about it and she stopped that."

I cooked a large dinner—one of his favorites. Filet mignon, mashed potatoes (mashed with a few milk-cooked leeks) and sautéed mushrooms.

He's taking a glass of wine again. What utter insanity to deny an 88-year-old man his wine. Even if it kills him, at least it would be a respectable demise as opposed to the alternatives of forced feeding and constant medication.

We, or rather I, talked about books and the world. And he was responsive and never faded once, although he rubbed his eyes constantly. It's the blind eye that troubles him most.

"It's terrible to lose one's sight. I'm deaf and now I can't see—it's awful. Not to be able to listen to anything and now not to be able to read. For someone who lives in the intellect, it is terrible. I've been having hallucinations, apparitions. So real that I sit up in bed and hold out my hand only to realize that I imagined the person. I'd rather have the prose than the poetry..."

I reminded him once again what his friend had said: "This is your mountain now."

There was a new lithograph on the wall and Henry asked me if I would like one.

"It has a tropical feeling, Henry. The colors are so intense and brilliant, like you painted it at high noon under a hot sun."

Brenda stayed for dinner and S left. Referring to the film rights argument, Henry said, "Well, everyone's lining up and playing their part. I'm the old author getting ready to die."

Brenda interrupted him and asked, "What's my part?" and Henry looked at her and said, "Oh you, you're the expensive call girl." Everyone was shocked, and Bill jumped right in and said, "What's my role, Henry?" and Henry responded, "Oh, you're the artist Bill." I refrained from asking what my role was.

I picked up the pictures a friend of Henry's took of the two of us. I'm delighted to have them. They will go to *The Michigan Quarterly*, which is publishing a transcript of the NPR interview that I did with Henry in honor of his 88th birthday. Alas, Henry isn't reading or answering his mail anymore. His eyes are failing him, as is everything else in his body.

March 1, 1980: Henry weakens daily. He is very frail now and his bones are like those of a bird. Last night I made a coq-au-vin for him. When I arrived, he was already sitting at the table, fidgeting and struggling to stay upright in his chair. I felt anger in him, actually for the first time, anger and frustration at his weakening powers. Yet, he continues to resist and defy the inevitability his years insist upon and nature demands. How tough he is. Tough, full of courage and dignity and intransigent pride.

I love him. He makes me feel appreciated. As a woman, as a human being and as a cook. He appreciates, acknowledges and respects what is good in a person, that which is best in a person. I never feel diminished in his presence; with Henry I feel at home, peaceful. It is not that he does not judge. He does judge, but it is an observant judging, one blended with wisdom and humanity and compassion.

When I went last night, I took peach blossoms from my tree for the table. Henry told me that he had planted fruit trees when he lived in Big Sur.

"What was so wonderful, Barbara, were the different colors. And then I'd come out of my little studio and pick a fig right off the tree. And it would be ripe and warm. Wonderful."

"My eyes are so bad. You have no idea how little I can see, Barbara." Yet I swear he looks right through me. The mind is still observant and penetrating. Even if he is stone cold blind I will always feel that he sees me.

He rubs his eyes constantly now. And at the dinner table last night his head slipped down inside his shoulders like a turtle. Then it slid towards the table, which it very nearly touched but didn't. Even when he falters, he holds himself up within the faltering. He slips but does not let go. He still refuses to give in, give up, give out. I hope he never stops refusing.

The head slips forward, a deep bending at the neck, his chin bowed nearly to his chest and then he raises his hands, both of them and places them gently on either side of his head. It is not that he holds his head but rather as if he is trying to steady it. It is a moment of repose.

Both hands at either side of his scalp, the long, delicate fingers slightly spread, the hair that remains soft and white, so soft I wanted to reach over and caress it, him, gather him up in my arms and hold him close.

Henry Miller: The Last Days

He is so frail and vulnerable, soft and hard at the same time, like a piece of jade, hard and soft, priceless and yet touchable, enduring, eternal, for all times and seasons and yet very much of the moment. He is an extraordinary human being.

Yet, an ordinary bloke as well, as Alfred Kazin wrote in the letter he sent to me. But extraordinary people are always ordinary close up because they don't need all the masks that the rest of us wear in an attempt to hide our very real ordinariness—because they know and accept themselves as they are. I'm not interested in the Henry of his earlier days. It is the Henry I know now that concerns me, not the Henry that Anaïs knew or anyone else for that matter.

Henry on Kenneth Patchen: "He was like a child with all the anger."

Henry is, in a way, a very Shakespearean character. We cannot fight against the world forever. It is fruitless and stupid to do so. The power of Shakespeare is his acceptance of all that man is.

S told me that the doctors think the seizures Henry is experiencing might be petit mal. At least he's not in any pain and, God willing, will go off in his sleep like his clown Auguste in *The Smile at the Foot of the Ladder*. He ends that slight book with:

> Perhaps I have not limned his portrait too clearly. But he exists, if only for the reason that I imagined him to be. He came from the blue and returns to the blue. He has not perished, he is not lost. Neither will he be forgotten.

Last night, when his head did literally drop onto his plate, Bill had to pick him up and physically hold and steady him. He just goes out and then when he comes back he picks up his sentence where he dropped off, and, of all things, he still frets about turning off the lights so as not to run up the electrical bills.

Alas, for better or worse, I'm about ready to move out of the Sherman Oaks Alomar house in the next few weeks into the small house that I bought in Studio City.

March 11, 1980: Last night was a good night at Henry's, as nights go these days. There were ten galleys for the Lawrence book and he gave me one, asking me to proofread it for him. While I'm delighted to do it, I think what he really wants to know is how I feel about the book. His hearing and eyesight worsen, but his appetite has been vigorous of late. He takes wine again with dinner and, as always, refuses to leave the table until he himself decides to do so. It doesn't matter that he fades off, rubs his eyes, drops his head in his plate, still he remains until he is ready to get up and go to bed.

Miller quoting Lawrence regarding the concept of friendship: "...I don't have friends who don't fundamentally agree with me. A friend means one who is at one with me in matters of life and death..." and "...man does not live by history or scientific law. The tree of life is sustained by faith and this faith is expressed in action."

And Henry, writing on that sentiment, says, "A noble attitude, now seemingly romantic, old-fashioned, because we are vitiated by indifference, because we are pragmatic and opportunistic. We subscribe to abstractions, principles, slogans, ideas, ideals—not to concrete flesh and blood. We talk big and act small. We are so flexible, so elastic, that we can play any tune at all. And the more abstract are our allegiances, the easier it is for us to evade responsibilities."

As Lawrence said, "Never let our own pride and courage of life be broken."

When I told Henry Ruth's comment that "Our faces are beginning to look like what we really are," he responded, "That's wonderful and quite a compliment too. Do you think so? Hmmm, I'm not so sure."

"Oh, yes, I do. It's beautiful."

March 16, 1980: Henry last night fingering his approaching death, walking around it so to speak, trying it on for size: "You think for the man of great spirit it should be a graceful thing, a just going to sleep. And yet that isn't necessarily true, you know. It could be awful, ignominious."

The bowel and bladder functions are gone. He falls constantly, the eyes and ears nearly gone, the world around him darker and darker. He trembles at the edge of the abyss, not sure whether to give in to the light that beckons him away from us or to stay on, clinging to the familiar disorders and disabilities that now beset him.

He is wearing a whiplash collar around his neck to steady it and to keep his head from drooping forward. He spoke about Brenda to me, saying, "I'm supposed to be a man in love, yet I won't see or talk to her. I don't want her to see me like this."

He told me that I was one of the "abnormal" in the same sense that he speaks of himself, of Lawrence, of those forever hopelessly and yet determinedly seeking after the spiritual. Quite a compliment.

April 17, 1980: Bill Pickerill said they had consulted a "healer" about Henry. The healer was unable to come but asked them to describe the symptoms, which they did. His response was that it sounded as if Henry were dying and there was nothing he could do about it.

Last Friday Henry brought up the subject again. Both seriously and with humor. The latter instance involved the wine, or rather the lack of it.

"It seems to me that a dying man should at least be allowed his glass of wine," Henry complained.

I asked Bill to give it to him then. Noel Young came for dinner, bringing someone who was unannounced along with him.

April 26, 1980: Henry last night not knowing the word "void." I saw the words written on his pad, on his newest watercolor as well—also fuck the duck—the void. Yet at dinner when I was telling him about Bill saying to me, "What's that?" Henry could not relate to the word. "I can't get it. I don't know what it is… I don't get it… Well, my dear Barbara, I have to take leave of you now."

In May of 1980, one month before Henry died, the Rumanian-born playwright Eugene Ionesco was in Los Angeles participating in a three-day symposium at the University of Southern California devoted to and in honor of his work. I was conducting an interview with him for National Public Radio[15] and in the course of our meetings I mentioned that I knew Miller. Ionesco was eager to meet Henry for whom he had great admiration and asked if I could arrange a meeting.

No two men could have been more different. Ionesco all doubt and despair, fixed on the contradictions, consumed by anguish; Miller, all accepting, preaching surrender, abdication and a self-created paradise, pure light. Yet they shared a reciprocal esteem for each other's work. Their starting point was similar, their roads different.

One of Henry's adages: "Those who think with the heart see life as a tragedy while those who perceive it with their heads see it as a comedy."

The meeting never occurred. Henry demurred, saying, "I don't want him to see me like this, how I am now." And then he added a few minutes later, "If Ionesco could see me now, that's something he could write a play about." Instead I took a set of books inscribed to Ionesco from Henry.

Moshe Lazar, a professor at USC, who acted as translator for me with Monsieur Ionesco, told me that when Ionesco heard about the Six Day War in Israel, he ran out of his Paris apartment and got drunk. Then he sat down in a chair in the middle of the street crying and lamenting and espousing his thoughts about the war.

When I repeated this to Henry, he said, "We can't do things like that here. It's amazing. Europeans can, but we Americans cannot."

It's the difference between "loving" man and finding him despicable. Henry sees man as he is and accepts that he is ridiculous but also allows the concept of nobility, greatness of spirit, beauty, love, joy to permeate his being. Ionesco doesn't allow himself to be touched by the possibility of these things. In response to my question regarding the light between the shadows, Ionesco said, "Well, it is so rare that we can't allow ourselves to build upon that as a structure." But like Henry, each in their own way, Ionesco believed that "Love is a state of Grace."

All these years later as I write about Henry I recall one of my favorite Ionesco quotes: "Above all one must not let oneself disintegrate. One must endure, resist, keep on living."

I keep this quote on an index card on my desk and in my heart.

May 3, 1980: Last night Henry was wonderful. He rallied to the conversation about Ionesco and never faltered once the entire meal.

May 15, 1980: I went for dinner with Henry tonight. I didn't write about him last week although I meant to jot down a few things. When I arrived in the late afternoon, the place was swarming with people. A French television crew was there to complete a documentary started a year earlier. Crew, cameras, lights, cables, boxes everywhere, along with the debris of empty beer cans, half-eaten sandwiches forgotten on waxed paper and brown paper bags.

When I arrived Bill was beside himself because of the crew and the general disruption for which no one was prepared. "It's such a violation. I can hardly wait until they leave."

"I won't be alive by dinner time; I'll be dead by then, Bill," Henry announced. He managed, however, to recover sufficiently to make it to dinner, which was an hour late as a result of all the commotion.

Twinka Thiebaud, one of Henry's best secretary-assistants and the author of a book of Henry's reminiscences titled *Reflections*, was there for dinner as well with her new baby, Sierra, cradled in her arms. The baby has beautiful dark eyes that are already a woman's eyes, rich, tawny skin and a lovely disposition. With no self-consciousness whatsoever, Twinka nursed her in front of everyone. Unlike most women who do this, she was graceful and discreet. The daughter of the painter Wayne Thiebaud, Twinka did not marry the father of the baby and refuses to live with him although they still see one another and share the child as well.

As Henry did not appear until dinnertime, the frustrated crew filmed every room in the house and virtually every painting on the premises. S had arranged the session without telling anyone and had conveniently removed herself to Palm Springs before they arrived. Bill told me that it was necessary in that Henry needed the money, that he was virtually without any cash and that he was getting about $50,000 for the project. (This might or might not be the case with so many "cooks" stirring the pot!)

Bill also told me S had turned down an offer of $400,000 two years earlier for the filming of *Sexus*. According to Bill, she advised Henry not to sell the rights as he would only end up with $200,000, the rest going to taxes. Whether or not this is the case, I have no idea. But it sounds ridiculous to me. Not that Bill would deliberately lie, but his dislike of S, his disgust and contempt, color his vision. It's hard to believe that she'd be such a fool, yet anything is possible in her drugged, somnambulist state.

The crew left in the late afternoon, and after dinner Henry gave me a new lithograph, one with a strange creature bearing the name Sarasota on the bottom of the picture. This is one of the last watercolors Henry produced and shows the figure of a man looking off to the right, a female figure looking straight ahead and, between the two, a diminutive male figure sketched in blue mimicking the pose of the larger male. Scattered around the painting is the usual Miller iconography: a Jewish star, squibbles locked into masses of red paint and blurbs of color suggestive of a dove, a fish...

Underneath all of this was a four-legged, grimacing beast with the name *Sarasota* written inside its body. The beast's teeth are bared in a fierce grimace, and I have often thought that this was how Henry actually felt. A sort of self-portrait—a beast with bared teeth. Henry told me that he had no idea what Sarasota meant or referred to. And he could still not relate to the word "void," which also found its way into the late watercolors. When I asked him about Sarasota, he squinted up his eyes, scratched his head in perplexity and said, "I can't get it. I don't know what it is." Sarasota is a city in Florida on the Gulf Coast, and perhaps Henry was once there. Who knows? Bill would know. He's becoming Henry's archivist and is beginning to answer the mail for him. He even begins to sound like Henry.

It was an arduous meal with Bill periodically reaching over to hold up Henry's head. Dinners are ordeals these days. Yet one has to admire Henry's tenacity. Perhaps all of our tenacity. Just getting him from the walker to the table is a major undertaking.

Last week he cried out like a hurt child when Bill lifted him. He hurts all over. This week he seemed better and stayed at the table nearly two hours.

It's not that he's senile. He isn't. It's just that he can no longer keep up. One's heart goes out as he defies the palsy that sets his hands atremble. He refuses to put the spoon down, clutching it until the shaking passes and then goes on eating his ice cream as if nothing had happened.

These days, if you ask how he feels the answer is always "lousy" or "terrible." And as incapacitated as he is, as blind, still, when he was being rolled off to his bedroom, he stopped and noticed my skirt. A red madras floor-length skirt. Reaching forward he gathered up the hem in his hand, gently stroking the material with his other hand and exclaiming over how wonderful it was, saying how I always wore beautiful clothes.

And then tonight he asked if he'd given me the Sarasota print, which he had.

"Do you have *Boyhood with Gurdjieff*?[16] I told Bill we had to give you a copy..." When Bill returned, Henry insisted on signing it, which he did with tremendous effort, the script spidery and barely legible. Henry loves the book and wrote the preface for it. When I said goodnight to him, I told him I'd see him next week. He kissed me and said, "I hope so, Barbara."

Shortly before he died, Henry wrote a *To Whom It May Concern* letter for me to use in applying for grants:

As a writer—not a critic—I have the highest regard for the writings of Barbara Kraft. Though her output is not enormous, the quality of her work is such as to put her in the category of true feminine writers such as Lady Murasaki, Sappho, Anaïs Nin, with whom she was close friends and, let us say, the author of Wuthering Heights. What distinguishes her work from that of the more prominent female writers of our time is her innate literary taste, her passion and her womanliness. She is not trying to imitate famous men, be they poets or novelists. She is a woman through and through, truthful to the core and thoroughly alive and aware. In short, she is a writer for all time.

Henry Miller

[P.S.] Dear Barbara—Will this do? HM.

Heat is prostrating!!

May 18, 1980: Without Bill there, Henry would be dead already. He is wonderful with Henry. Warm and protective and loving. He never talks down to him or otherwise diminishes him. He loves Henry, truly loves him. Again, I can only wonder about Bill's own father. He's never spoken a word about his background, his family, where he came from. Perhaps because it never occurred to me to ask; we're both so involved with Henry there's no thought of anything else. The only thing we have in common is Henry and his well-being.

What a week this has been for me. Carlos Fuentes, Mexico's ambassador to France, at the University of Southern California on Monday, the Beverly Sills recital at Crystal Cathedral in Garden Grove on Tuesday,

Henry Miller: The Last Days

Wednesday an Amnesty International meeting, Thursday and Friday Amnesty's benefit.

I just spoke with Bill. Henry is rapidly failing. Totally disoriented as to the time of day, unable to express himself, put words into a coherent sentence. He wants a bath in the middle of the night and breakfast at 2 p.m. The palsy in his hands is increasing.

May 23, 1980: Very bad night for Henry last night. He could barely sit up. An ordeal but somehow not sad. He is so much connected to life, to realness, that this too seems appropriate, part of "his" natural process.

May 27, 1980: I went to Henry's for dinner on Friday and spent all day yesterday at his house. Memorial Day. Very trying, to say the least. He's just not there most of the time. A part of the brain is gone, or sections connecting one part with another have short-circuited. When words come out of his mouth, they come out fragmented, with no beginning and no ending; they just hang awkwardly in space.

He tries to say something, but what comes out has no relationship to anything that has been going on. After a few garbled words, he is lost, bewildered, dropping his head to his chest, a position he will stay in for an unbearable length of time while the rest of us look on anxiously, waiting for the slow raising of his head.

When he does bring his head up, almost as if he were coming up for air, he fixes you with a bewildered look and says, "Isn't that the damnedest thing" and shakes his head sadly. He knows he's slipping away, that he's not all there. He fears that he is going mad. Bill told me he had dictated letters to his friends Lawrence Durrell and Alfred Perlès, to Brenda expressing this fear...

"I think I'm going mad. I'm afraid I'm losing my mind."

Friday night I was there with only Barry to help me. Most of the meal Henry sat with his head falling in his plate. When Barry did manage to pull his head up and get the collar round his neck, he would look around at us as if he were lost in a dream, trying to figure out where he was. He couldn't even hold the fork, dropping it and his hands into his plate, spittle dribbling constantly from his mouth. And sadly, he was aware of this.

He constantly fingers his napkin, trying to raise his hands to wipe his mouth. The hands are nervous beings, creatures independent from him, struggling to fold and unfold his napkin. A heroic gesture under the circumstances. He accepts his condition, but he does not give in to it.

There was no conversation whatsoever. Last night was better, however. For some reason he rallied sufficiently to try to hold a conversation with me. I saw him looking at us and watching as we chatted about nothing, Bill, Twinka and myself. And I had the sense that he felt terribly left out. At one point he looked at me and asked, "Are you talking about me?" I was sitting across from him in the guest's chair of better days.

"No, Henry, we're not." And then I tried to include him in the conversation.

He fixed me with that open-eyed attention of his, and with a bewildered expression on his face he shook his head sadly and said, "It's been like an adventure these past two or three days. I don't know where I am, where

Henry Miller: The Last Days

this place is, what this house is—it's the damnedest thing."

"It's your house, Henry," I explained. "And I've been here all day, sitting out by the pool."

"The pool? There's a swimming pool here?"

"Yes."

"Were there other people here?"

"Yes. Bill and Barry, S and myself."

"That's all. What a shame. Weren't there others?"

"No. It's your pool, Henry, not a public one."

"Mine?" he said, with great surprise.

"Yes, yours. You own it."

"You don't say. I own it!"

"Yes and this house too."

"Amazing!"

Then he rubbed his eyes and ran his hands over his head, a familiar caressing gesture by now, smoothing his long-lost hair. And he continually attempted to adjust his hearing aid. As if he could tune the world back in and rub away the fog and confusion that besets him.

Henry had never been overwhelmed by the burden of disillusion but this was another time and space…and even so he never admitted defeat.

There were mornings when Henry awoke from a dream that he was back in the Paris streets of the 1930s, hungry and penniless, asking anyone who came into his room if there was any money in his wallet, in theirs, for breakfast as he was famished.

And a few days before he died he woke up asking Barry for his wallet. "I'm really hungry for breakfast. Can you find my wallet for me? I've looked everywhere for it."

"Here it is, Henry."

"Is there any money in it?"

"I'll look. No, Henry. There's no money in it. None at all."

"What are we going to do for breakfast? I'm really hungry this morning."

Barry assured him that he would stand him for breakfast. "You don't need to worry, Henry. I'll pay for breakfast today. I have some money."

Henry was not about to give up yet. He was in no way ready to relinquish the little patch of life left to him. While he could no longer read the newspapers, he adamantly maintained the habit of it, holding it more often than not upside down at the breakfast table, refusing to relinquish it or to allow anyone to turn it right side up.

Still, the news of the day somehow managed to filter through where it metamorphosed into wild, chaotic tales in his dreams. He regaled us all one evening with a story of how he had been blindfolded and abducted from a movie theater by the Iranians earlier in the day. "It's been like an adventure," he rambled on, his mind a jumble of strange images. Most likely he had picked this up from watching the television or trying to watch. It must be like a movie in his head. He constantly refers to the Iranians.

And then he was trying to tell me about two movies he had recently seen, but of course he hasn't seen a movie in years.

Henry Miller: The Last Days

While he and I talked, Twinka motioned to Bill to get the tape recorder, which annoyed me. I hated their rushing to preserve every garbled fragment that issued from his mouth. But then, what I am doing writing it all down, chapter and verse? The whole thing is so funny and sad and macabre and marvelous. Henry is the most stubborn man I have ever met. For me, Henry has redefined the notion of courage—it is one's refusal to be overcome by life. What did he say to me last night in answer to one of my questions about how it feels to be him now? "Well, we must accept what comes, don't you know?"

That "don't you know" was the first one I'd heard from him in weeks and I wanted to hug and kiss him, laugh and cry.

Henry frequently falls out of bed at night and is a mass of bruises and sores; he cries out in pain when they lift him from bed to stroller to the chair, yet the ritual of dinners continues. His words come out garbled, his thoughts fragmented and undecipherable, and there are long, impenetrable silences.

And just as he refuses to give up the newspaper, so too he won't relinquish the dinners. It is a super-human feat to get him to the table these days for all concerned, including Henry himself.

Last night again, the serious effort to fold his napkin and insert it into his silver monogrammed napkin holder demanded all his attention. I'll never forget the business with the napkin, one tiny island of control that he can still master. And master it he does.

With all of this transpiring, it wasn't sad in that house, at that table, in that bathroom. Touching, yes. And moving. And immensely human and funny too. We were not laughing at him. Our laughter was mixed with tears, like the sun breaking through the center of an intermittent deluge.

What extraordinary things must be going through his mind now.

Nearing the end, a crazy strength coursed through Henry's failing form, the terrible energy of the dying. The other night he forgot that he can no longer walk and managed to get as far as the hall before he fell down. He cut his head and his elbow, bruising the entire right side of his body. And on another night, he managed to get into the bathroom where he closed the door before collapsing. Bill happened to pass by the hall and noticed that the bathroom door was closed, although there was no light coming from under the door. He managed to open the door, which was not locked but had jammed against the shower door.

The bathroom, as legendary as his lists and charts and part of the Miller lore, was covered floor to ceiling with photographs of friends, naked women, idols such as Nietzsche, Emerson and Lawrence and gurus like Krishnamurti and Gurdjieff. When he was found by Bill, Henry was sitting on the floor in the middle of the bathroom, gesticulating and talking to some image on the wall, calling, "Monsieur, Monsieur." According to Bill, Henry looked up calmly and said, "Oh, Bill, I'm so glad to see you again. How good that you're passing by just now. I'm having the damnedest time with this guy."

And so it was not illogical, given the state of his mind that he would engage in conversation with some fading face from the past.

He then related the efforts that got him where he was. "I had to take a leak so I tried to turn on the light over my bed (there's a bottle for him to pee into next to his bed). I couldn't reach it and I thought I'll get up and go to the bathroom. I tried to find the light on the wall but I couldn't find the switch. When I got to the bathroom, I couldn't find that light either. So here I am. How good of you to come by."

It's all a crazy mix of fact and fantasy, of fragmented reality, and if Henry could write it he would do so with delight for he was a man at peace with himself. He had acted out and lived his beliefs.

A little more than a week before Henry died he received the following letter from one of his dearest and oldest friends Alfred Perlès; it was a "goodbye" letter of sorts—from Joey to Joey—dated May 23, 1980, 15 days before Henry's death on June 7:

> Dear Henry,
>
> I don't know what to make of that strange letter I had the other day which, its writer claims, was dictated by you. But can that be true? I don't recognize *you* in this extraordinary missive, it's not the kind of letter you'd normally write and there's no trace of your style in it. It's written on your note-paper but there's no clue to the person's name who wrote the letter. It wasn't Tony, of that I'm sure, for Tony is a better speller

than the chap who wrote under your dictation (?). I'm full of doubts.

What the letter implies is that you're on the point of dying, though the words actually used are that you're "leaving the planet." Well, Joey, you're not going to leave the planet, no matter what you do, even [if] you die and are cremated, for even then the smoke that has been your physical entity won't get out of the precinct of the planet. But hair-splitting aside, let me tell you in so far as I (and probably a few million others) am concerned, you won't be dead, even if you do die. That's why I'm not to be counted among the mourners.

A few weeks ago, Bertrand Mathieu sent me a snapshot of you and him taken six months ago. You look a bit frail in it but still quite alive. You've been through a lot of physical pain and being blind in one eye and deaf in [one] ear is a severe handicap. Yet you seem to have suffered in silence and clung to life. In a way, you remind me of Marshal Tito who died after having for months been on the point of dying. Aren't we all on the point of dying? For months or for years, what's the difference? So in case you do go the way of all flesh I shan't miss you, Joey, simply because what's essential in you cannot leave me ever.

So bon voyage, Joey, and auf Wiedersehen, in Devachan or anywhere else where they decant good vintage wines.

Fred

P.S. Can you give me Tony's address?

Henry Miller: The Last Days

Saturday, June 7, 1980: Henry died today. When the end came it wasn't awful, it wasn't ignominious. It all happened very simply and was just short of a "going to sleep." Henry died at home in his own bed in the arms of Bill Pickerill on a Saturday afternoon at 4:35 p.m.

June 15, 1980: Dear Henry, we are laying you to rest today. And yes, in a public ceremony—over the radio—a four-hour salute over KCRW. Lux Aeterna, Henry. No Requiem Mass for you. Rather a Ceremony of Light and Music. We are playing the music that you chose for your 87th birthday celebration, December 1978.[17]

I end this memoir with Miller's own words—words that I copied out and hung on my mirror to buoy my spirits in the mornings.

Paradise is everywhere and every road, if one continues along it far enough, leads to it. One can only go forward and then sideways and then up and then down. There is no progress: there is perpetual movement, displacement, which is circular, spiral, endless. Every man has his own destiny; the only imperative is to follow it, to accept it, no matter where it leads him... Understanding is not piercing of the mystery but an acceptance of it, a living blissfully with it, in it, through and by it.

Barbara Kraft

For Immediate Release June 9, 1980

KCRW SALUTES HENRY MILLER

KCRW presents a special 4-hour SALUTE TO HENRY MILLER Sunday, June 15, beginning at 3 p.m. The legendary writer died last Saturday at his home in Pacific Palisades.

The program will highlight a conversation with Miller especially recorded for KCRW by writer Barbara Kraft on the occasion of his 88th birthday last December. Miller remembered his "joyous misery"—those Paris years he worked on the *Tropics*. Ms. Kraft, a close friend in his last years, describes his way of life, the household routine of rotating cooks, recounts his conversations and conveys the spirit that animated his last works of art.

The broadcast will include a concert of selections that Miller himself chose, ranging from Wagner's "Liebestod" to Fats Waller's "Two Sleepy People."

KCRW 89.9 FM is a National Public Radio affiliate in Santa Monica College.

SPECIAL

APPENDIX

An Open Letter to Henry Miller (1977)

Dear Henry Miller:

I am a long time, serious, I mean I've read all the work, and ardent, meaning I love the work, fan of yours although I've never allowed myself the liberty of writing to you. Still, for a considerable time I have wanted to do so. Now comes this opportunity.

Saturday, three to five, Henry Miller "Questions and Answers." Five foot-eight, perhaps less, a slight but enduring frame, delicate but tenacious like the white prayer trees of Japan, gray suit (reminding one that you are of the Bogart generation), red-checkered shirt, kerchief carefully folded in lapel pocket, white socks, fluffy white bedroom slippers, a carved cane…again slender but sturdy. A slow crossing from the wings to the chair, table, microphone, water glass…on the arm of your friend Jack Garfein who was moderating the event…cane in the other hand, but not an old man.

No! You'll never be old. Age cannot touch you. I defy you to become old. I don't recall a wrinkle in your face and even though your hands were heavily veined and purple, still, somehow, they too defy age, looking bruised rather than old. You have quite simply evolved into being more and more the being Henry Miller. I was enchanted, charmed and totally satisfied. You were as I had come to know you through your books. I had finally seen Miller the man, and wonder of wonders; he matched the Miller of the page.

Rare that. The man and the work are often two very different things. I had been afraid that in the flesh you might let me down. Might be but a pale hint of the work, the half moon behind the sun. But no! You and your work fit together like two halves of the same shell. A shell with the luster of the sun, full of light. The naturalness, the straight-ahead and direct prose, the clean simplicity, the lack of affectation or pomposity, the affirmation of tone, the humor and wit, the flow of the born story-teller, in short, the unbeatable spirit of the man. All of those qualities which light up the page for me lit up the stage that day.

"Does the young lady down there in white have a question for me?" A gentle laughter, a soft breeze through the 100 gathered.

Miller doing, being what people have come to think of him as doing, as being. Miller giving them what they want with the boyish charm of a man who truly reveres and loves women. In spite of how you have written about women, the feeling remains strong in me that you like women, admire them. Are even in awe of them. Am I mistaken?

As you sat there, taking questions through a "translator" because of your diminished hearing, I realized the importance of your creed of acceptance. For by accepting what is, we do indeed transcend it, and with our dignity intact. Once we stop struggling against and accept, then all becomes part of one long, continuous, eternal flow.

"Paradise is everywhere and every road, if one continues along it far enough, leads to it. One can only go forward and then sideways and then up and then down.

There is no progress: there is perpetual movement, displacement, which is circular, spiral, endless. Every man has his own destiny: the only imperative is to follow it, to accept it, no matter where it leads him... Understanding is not piercing of the mystery but an acceptance of it, a living blissfully with it, in it, through and by it."

Question: What form of government do you think best for the artist to live under?

Answer: No government!

In the American Grain. That is how I think of you. Never as an expatriate. Never urbane like Fitzgerald or macho like Hemingway. And, in fact, though you were in Paris during the days of the Stein salon, you were never a part of it. You were much more of an intellectual than were they. American in the true sense of the word. Following in the tradition of Whitman, Thoreau, Emerson and standing for all those things we as a country are supposed to be about.

Stubborn individualists, men of the open land, of the open road, men not stopped by the limits of the horizon or the government. Mavericks, pioneers who pushed beyond, seers who saw what could be, what this land could become. Romantics, all of them, and you as well, but not in the European sense of that word which implies unfulfilled longing, a yearning for the absolute, for the summit, for the unattainable, a longing that finds its fulfillment, its consummation only in death. No, you are not of that tradition. Nor were the others, Whitman, Thoreau, Emerson. The American romanticists were singers. Singing romantics even when the song rang out harsh and strident.

Prophets, all of you, of what has come to pass. For they were against government and for the individual, for life. They transcended, glorified, reveled in life. You identified all with Lawrence's term "aristocrats of the spirit."

Their message, like yours, is one of affirmation. Even when you're raging, the rage is like a clarion ringing for life. The rage is filled with a living, breath, vibrant vitality.

Boundaries are not accepted; there are no barriers. Not even evil. Anarchists...a faith born of love, dream, pure phenomena... Walden... Man should be the harp articulate... Afoot and light-hearted I take to the open road. You are of the same stuff as Whitman and Thoreau. Emerson, too. The words you use to describe them fit you as well. A cloth cut to the same size.

A spangled garment to wrap around those who have learned to *Stand Still Like the Hummingbird.*

Despite the absence of any visible imprimatur, such as a Nobel or a Pulitzer, your day will come and you will be exalted as have been Whitman and Thoreau and Emerson. It's hard to believe that you've never been publicly honored by any of the honoring institutions in this country.

But then the true artist never does fit into the busy-bee, clock-time society in which he finds himself. He is anti-social by nature and against by creed, by religion, by conscience, against all that is and the average man takes comfort in.

As you write:

We are in the Time of the Assassins. The order of the day is: liquidate! The enemy, the arch-enemy, is the man who speaks the truth. Every realm of society is permeated with falsity and falsification. What survives, what is upheld, what is defended to the last ditch is the lie.

"...Here in my opinion is the only imaginative prose writer of the slightest value who has appeared among the English-speaking races for some years past," George Orwell wrote in *Inside the Whale*, his 1940 essay on you.

"Even if that is objected to as an overstatement, it will probably be admitted that Miller is a writer out of the ordinary, worth more than a single glance; and after all, he is a completely negative, unconstructive, amoral writer, a mere Jonah, a passive acceptor of evil...a sort of Whitman among the corpses."

This appraisal was predicated on the books you had published to date in the '30s—obviously written in response to the *Tropic* books, which were published in 1934 and 1939; in between was *Black Spring*, 1936.

Art, by definition, breaks down barriers and that is just what you did. The *Tropic* books shattered the world.

A letter from Lawrence Durrell:

Dear Henry Miller: I have just read Tropic of Cancer again and I feel like I'd like to write you a line about it. It strikes me as being the only really man-size piece of work which this century can really boast of. It's a howling triumph from the word go; and not only is it a literary and artistic smack on the bell for everyone, but it really gets down on paper the blood and bowels of our time. I have never read anything like it. I did not imagine anything like it could be written; and yet, curiously, reading it I seemed to recognize it as something which I knew we were all ready for. The space was all cleared for it. Tropic turns the corner into a new life which has regained its bowels.

Question: What do you think of pornography?
Answer: I did not write pornography. That is something else. What I wrote is may be erotic...but not pornography..."that dirty old man who wrote all those dirty books..." I know that's what they say of me.

I know you didn't write dirty books. The whole world knows you didn't write dirty books. What you did was to write life. And I often found myself very aroused by the life you wrote. As you said somewhere, you brought life back into literature. And I agree.

When I am at my lowest moments, I find it is to you that I turn for sustenance, for renewal of faith, for belief in myself, in mankind. For even when you are critical and outrageous, nevertheless, you remain a celebrant of life.

My favorites are *The Colossus of Maroussi, The Wisdom of the Heart, Stand Still Like the Hummingbird, The Air-Conditioned Nightmare, Big Sur and the Oranges of Hieronymus Bosch, The Cosmological Eye, Remember to Remember, Time of the Assassins*...

Within these pages an incredible range of people, places, thoughts, visions, swim like a school of electric fish in the sea of your prose. Rising and falling, sweeping one along in the rich tide of your ideas. You were a man with only one story to write. Your own! And write it you did, embellishing and ornamenting as you went along. Redemption, salvation, faith, art, religion, mysticism, happiness, acceptance and above all else, life, living here and now, in the present, not over there, not over some hill or at the end of some rainbow.

At the "foot of the ladder," however. You will *Smile at the Foot of the Ladder* before you leave terra firma. When I said earlier that I love the work, what I meant was that I love the spirit of the man that leaps off the page, singes the edges of my heart and brands my soul with the emblem of life itself.

Question: Have you ever known loneliness?
Answer: Yes, I guess I have. In the Big Sur period. But I reveled in it.

Question: Do you think that you were able to do that, to revel in it, because you accepted the loneliness as the condition of your existence at the moment?
Answer: Yes, I think so.

But surely you were not always of such an insouciant nature. How did all those books get written? Or were you? Anaïs told me that she had never seen you depressed or despondent. Rather always laughing, joyous, full of life, buoyant, joking, telling stories. Where does that spirit come from? And it's still there, that indefatigable spirit. As I speak to you a moth ponders the impenetrability of the glass separating him from the light...much as I ponder your nature. I am able to see it, feel it, but struggle to grasp it in my hands. It eludes me, beckoning me back into the pages of your books. The answers are there. Back to the beginning.

The nascent writer. Paris. The Miller-Nin correspondence. The early '30s. I walk through your words and across the pages of print to better finger your soul. The letters were in reality a journal, written as much to yourself as to Anaïs, who was overwhelmed by their sheer volume, often twenty pages in length, so she told me.

A mind on the road, inflamed, thirsty, in search of the Holy Grail. You send her detailed notes as to what you are reading: Rilke, Lawrence, Spengler, Nietzsche, Dostoyevsky, Cendrars, Tristan Tzara, Joyce, Chirico, Proust. The mind like a beehive and inside the honeycomb: *"God, it is maddening to think that even one day must pass without writing. I shall never, never catch up. And it is no doubt why I write with such vehemence, such distortion. It is despair... God, I feel that I am somebody, a force, a necessity—and by some delicious irony, I find I am planted in a desert, on an absolutely futile, ridiculous errand..."*

Proust went to your head and Dostoyevsky as well.

Dear Anaïs... Have just left the cinema after seeing "City Lights" with profound conviction that Chaplin is great... Dear Anaïs: When you asked if I thought my writing might be interpreted as erotic, I must say yes, but that isn't enough. Just yes! I don't think of it as being defined by this or that, as representing this or that. I am trying to be a man, to speak as a man speaks and not to leave out anything because of principles, art, or whatever it may be that has constrained men heretofore. And I write in the first person in order to get close to verisimilitude—not for the sake of realism... I lie occasionally—why not? My lying is in keeping with giving the truth about myself. It is not a machine that is registering this record of a soul, but a human being.

And a postscript from another letter: *The best thing in Dada was "God can afford to make mistakes. So can Dada." (That's a very old idea of mine.)*

Henry Miller: The Last Days

And recalling the legend of you as the starving artist, a reality that time has worked into the tapestry of your lengthy years: *Anaïs: Got your letter shortly after telephoning. The 100 francs came in damned handy. I was walking around in Fred's patent leather shoes which didn't fit me and caught a fresh cold changing from his shoes to my thin sandals. Anyway, I just bought a stout pair of workingmen's shoes here in Clichy. They asked me if I worked in the quarter. I said yes. Nice to be taken for an ouvrier instead of a rich American.*

And they go on and on, these remarkable letters, until you left Paris and went to Greece. To avoid the war? There has been much speculation about the question of the role of the artist in society. Or does he have a role? There are those, and you are one of them, who believe that the artist's only duty is to himself and that by serving himself he ultimately serves mankind.

The Colossus of Maroussi is a case in point. You glorified the Greek spirit, the violet light, the huge boulders, the hard land...all of this you did and wrote about at a time when the Greeks themselves were starving to death and nary a word of that. In fact, you suggested that the only food they needed was spiritual food.

No less a figure than Kazantzakis took issue with the Greece of your depiction, writing, *Poverty, when it is not excessive and does not reach the point of hunger and misery, is really well suited to any people or any individual averse to weighing the spirit down with the flesh. But when poverty is excessive, it becomes a blight that degrades man. In Greece the poverty is excessive. According to official statistics, 2,300,000 Greeks—that is one third of the population—do not eat when they are hungry.*

It is shameful to remain unperturbed by so tragic a situation. The writer, who is by nature more sensitive, cannot repress his indignation or shirk his responsibility. He is duty-bound not to sleep; he must keep his people on alert. Furthermore, I think that this role of the writer as agitator is indispensable in all countries ruled by injustice. I mean to say, virtually throughout the whole earth.

And yet, despite the validity of what he says, *The Colossus of Maroussi* remains one of the most inspirational books I've ever read. What if you and Kazantzakis had met? Kazantzakis too wrote of simple men—Zorba, Saint Francis, Christ. His simple men were out to save the souls of other men. But you were not interested in saving souls. East meeting West? A reversal of roles. For although Kazantzakis called himself a man of the East, he was Western, Germanic even, in his thought. Whereas your mentality is one of "an ease of acceptance," a mentality decidedly more Eastern than Western.

What would your answer have been? Perhaps this passage on saviors: *For these active spirits the light of truth proved not only blinding but shattering. In ways unpremeditated and unforeseen they activated the soul of man. And in their wake strife and conflict multiplied. Man was regenerated, not made over: he became the battleground of darker, more disturbing forces. And so, regardless of their heroic behavior, regardless of their sublime motives, I have come to regard such activity as indefensible. Even from the purest of motives one has not the right to "molest" another.*

The effort to bring a man to God, or to bring him enlightenment, is an act of violation. It is even more reprehensible than to subjugate him bodily. Does not the whole art of living center about the practice of tolerance, or noninterference? Before it is possible to love one another, as we are so often enjoined, it is necessary to respect one another, the privacy of the soul.

Well, enough of that. It is an idea that has interested me for some time. There is no one answer, of course. It is enough to flush out the thought, the idea every once in a while and hope that people will care enough to line up behind the position that rings truest for them.

Dear Mr. Miller, it grows late. The moon has crossed the sky while I have been scribbling. Have I succeeded in showing some of your many selves? A man has many faces. He does not show them all. In conclusion, then: You achieved what you set out to achieve. You wrote as a man, as a man thinks and speaks, you charged literature with a new life, hooking it in to the powerful voltage of your soul by daring to write the life as I. The sheer force of energy propelling the words across and down page after page is dizzying, exciting, a spinning, reeling sensation. An incredible high.

And you succeeded as well in arriving at a vision that transcends conflict, one that does not look upon an idea as one being right and the other wrong. Your vision embraces the two. Thus, although there are polarities in your thought, I never come away with a sense of conflict or tension or feel that you are at odds with the I within the You. Rather I leave your books with a feeling of vision of peace, of renewal, of affirmation and often exaltation.

As I wrote above, a man has many faces. Let me try to flush out some the faces that come to my mind and fix you in my sensibilities. The eternal singer—sometimes out-of-tune, off-key—who nevertheless revels in singing for the pure act that it is; the clown "in season and out"; the celebrant at the altar of life; an earth digger in the tradition of Rabelais but never that of a de Sade.

And although you think of yourself in Buddha-like terms, I do not. The twinkle in the eye, the slightly wry grin, the vitality—all conspire to deny you that mirror. I see you ultimately as a contented dove on its roost, peacefully folding its wings in acceptance over the dualities of the now resolved warring selves. In the sense that art is something that points toward a spiritual action, a way of making us feel and understand, think and exist, you have succeeded in capital letters. They should erect marquees, billboards all over this country lit up with these words of yours, for the world needs to remember that *the worst is not death but being blind, blind to the fact that everything about life is in the nature of the miraculous.*

henry miller 444 **ocampo** drive -- **pacific palisades** california 90272

Dear Barbara –   Dec. 24th 77

I listened to the cassette you sent me yesterday and was astounded, overwhelmed. You say this Barbara Kraft is a writer and that she gave this message over the radio. (Was it over the National Public Radio by chance?)

I am extremely curious about this woman. It was an extraordinary appraisal both of me and my work I thought. In fact I am getting several copies of it made. (Don't you want one for yourself?)

Tell her for me, if you see her again, that even Anaïs Nin could not have done as well as she.

If you have the time, send me her address and I will write and thank her. Thank *you* for sending it to me.

By the way, your painting won't get mailed until next week probably. Post office too crowded to go inside.

Have a good holiday!
         Love, Dad.

Letter from Henry Miller to his daughter Barbara

Postcard from Henry Miller to Barbara Kraft

henry miller 444 **ocampo** drive – **pacific palisades** california 90272

2/14/78

Dear Barbara Kraft —

I feel apologetic for holding your work so long but my sight is worse than ever and I have had to go at it very slowly. So here are a few things back. The book I haven't been able to look at yet. But first of all let me tell you what a truly remarkable writer you are. The piece on Van Gogh out of this world! The one on your father's death about as strong a thing as I ever read by anyone.

In your curriculum vitae I notice the great part music plays, or has played, in your life. You must know Zubin Mehta's father, don't you? I like him as a human being so much more than his brilliant son. Do you play the piano still? Do you improvise? I almost became a pianist rather than a writer or painter, but marrying at 10 and quit at 25.—that idea. Chopin at 10 and then—Today I listened only now and to do. Scriabin too—many other things. A great favorite (or his 5th Sonata) is my "Gaspard de la Nuit". With Ravel it's "Gaspard de la Nuit". Bach must confess I don't care for Bach at all!

When I do a little more reading I'll write you over for dinner again.

(over)

"HENRY, NOW AND THEN I MAY BE OBLIGED TO SLEEP IN MY CAR, BUT WHEN I NEED TO TAKE A SHIT I GO TO THE BEVERLY HILLS HOTEL."
(Florian Steiner)

Letter from Henry Miller to Barbara Kraft

To be honest, I think you are a greater writer than A.N. whom you refer to as your master. You have a better and a stronger command of the language, in my humble opinion. Anaïs was always timid due, I suppose, to speaking Spanish and French first. I never did agree with her, you know, about the importance she gives psycho-analysis.

By the way, I read (first of all) the thing about Him you gave over the radio. It is most excellent. You have lots of fire in you. I forgot to ask what are your natal and rising signs. (Could one be Scorpio?)

My sight is giving out — must stop. I'll pass the book on to Tony after I read the pages you clipped.

Shit! How stupid of me to overlook the subtitle of your book (Gemini). Tho' what whatever was also a Gemini, it seems to me there must be other factors to account for your vigor and depth. (My mother was a Gemini and like your father, a cold fish. Deliberately refused to read anything of mine — can you imagine?

Well, enough! All the best to you! Thank you for a great treat!

Henry Miller

Henry Miller: The Last Days

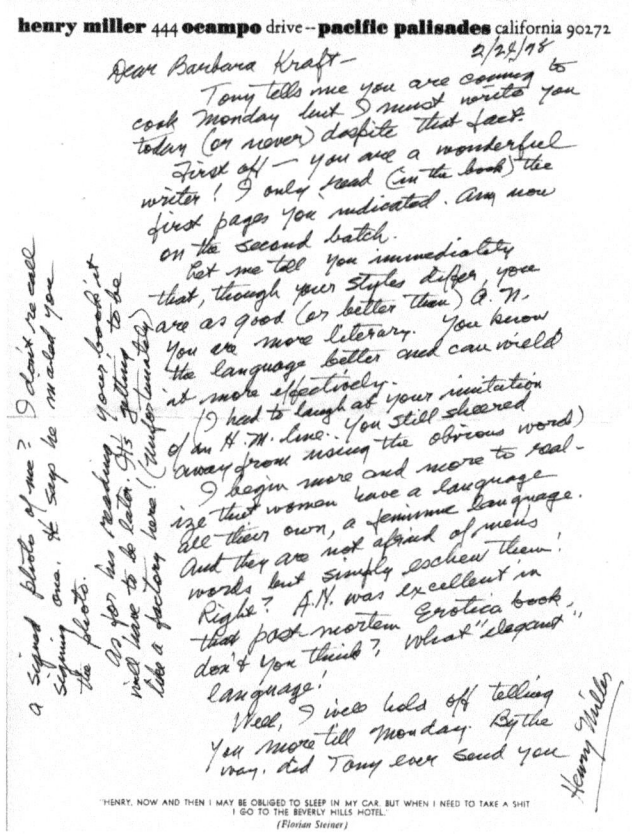

Letter from Henry Miller to Barbara Kraft

```
       VYB121(2010)(4-068893E054)PD 02/23/78 2010
ICS IPMRNCZ CSP
 2134544080 TDRN PACIFIC PALISADES CA 22 02-23 0810P EST
 PMS BARBARA KRAFT, DELIVER SOONEST, DLR
3681 ALOMAR DR
SHERMAN OAKS CA 91423
DEAR BARBARA,
HENRY WOULD LIKE TO KNOW IF YOU ARE AVAILABLE TO COOK THIS SATURDAY
   NIGHT PLEASE PHONE SOONEST 2134544080 OR 4595183
   TONY MILLER FOR HENRY MILLER
NNNN
```

Telegram from Tony Miller to Barbara Kraft

Dear Friend, Barbara Kraft

In my attempt to obtain the Nobel Prize for Literature this coming year I hope to enlist your support. All I ask is for you to write a few succinct lines to:

Nobel Committee of the Swedish Academy
Borshuset
11129 Stockholm
Sweden

Please note that the Committee urgently requests that the name of the proposed candidate not be publicized.

Sincerely,
Henry Miller

"WHEN LOVE COMES TO THE FORE WOMAN WILL BE THE QUEEN OF THE UNIVERSE" Eliphas Levi

Henry Miller's form letter for Nobel Prize

Henry Miller: The Last Days

> Saturday June 3, 1979
>
> Dear Barbara — Just a word to congratulate you on a marvelous dinner last night. That filet mignon was the tenderest and tastiest meat I have tasted in many a year. This morning I had the flan again. Out of this world. You are chef #1 on my list of 16 cooks. When do you leave for Arkansas? All the best always.
>
> Henry

Note from Henry Miller to Barbara Kraft

henry miller 444 **ocampo** drive – **pacific palisades** california 90272

6/6/79

Dear Barbara –

I don't think Stettner has ever published anything in this lingo of ▮▮. This language of his, tho' very special to a certain class, is real American talk. (To me belongs to cops and robbers more than mere street dialect.) I don't know what his reactions will be. I am writing him today about Larry – to reassure him he's not dealing with a plainclothes man. (Excuse me.)

Saras told me Saturday of what Bert Mathieu's mag did with your article on me. I am waiting to hear from him — since you wrote something (and much deserved) letter. Somehow I can't believe Bert did this. Believe one of the editors must have done it. We'll see. But you are dead right, never let any one print without first reading proof. I have been having similar trouble with my friend and publisher Noel Young. It can happen to any one!

Glad you're not leaving for that Arkansas trip, yet.

All the best!

Henry

"I PISS ON IT ALL FROM A CONSIDERABLE HEIGHT." L. F. Celine

Letter from Henry Miller to Barbara Kraft

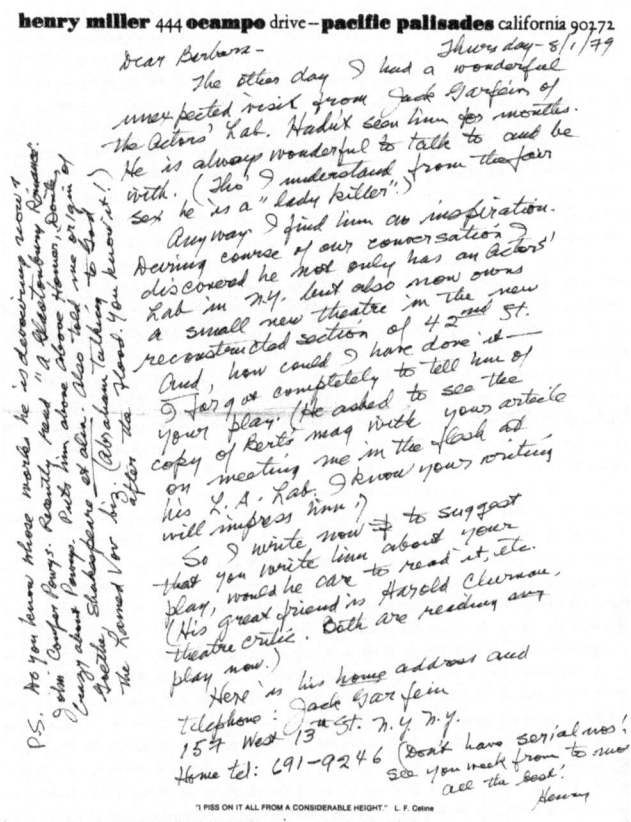

Letter from Henry Miller to Barbara Kraft

Barbara Kraft

> **henry miller** 444 ocampo drive–**pacific palisades** california 90272
>
> September 14, 1979
>
> To Whom it may concern:
>
> This is to verify that Barbara and Jennifer Kraft will be living with me at this address as of this date.
>
> *Henry Miller*
>
> Henry Miller

Henry Miller's letter to Pacific Palisades Schools

Henry Miller: The Last Days

henry miller 444 **ocampo** drive -- **pacific palisades** california 90272

12/4/79 Tuesday

Dear Barbara —

Was surprised to get your letter about N.P.R. today. Do you want me to write — damn (know exactly) and say I don't want it done — this way. How I did it with you and not an actor.

I don't give a damn about birthday celebrations. I think it's an insult to you. (How did your good friend Ruth let this happen.

They sure aren't doing me a favor. Perhaps they think they are. Ask Ruth to drop me a line about it.

I answered the loan biz. Hoped they would be more sociable with me.

Have a good Thanksgiving! It's coming to you!!! You sure deserve it.

cheers!

Henry

CUANDO MERDA TIVER VALOR POBRE NASCE SEM CU

Letter from Henry Miller to Barbara Kraft

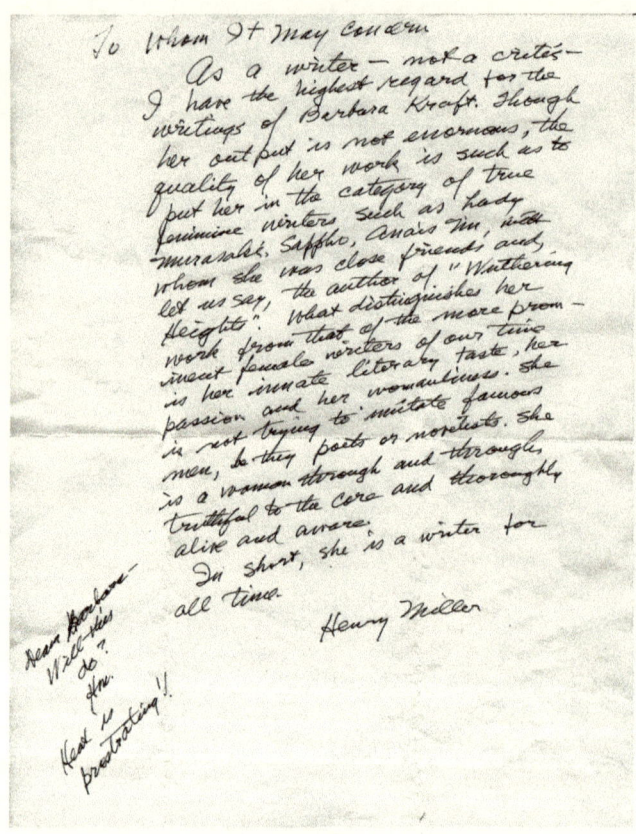

Henry Miller's recommendation letter for Barbara Kraft

Henry Miller: The Last Days

> 6, Spring Rise,
> Wells, Somerset BA5 1UB
>
> 23rd May, 1980.
>
> Dear Henry,
>
> I don't know what to make of that strange letter I had the other day which, its writer claims, was dictated by you. But can that be true? I don't recognise you in this extraordinary missive, it's not the kind of letter you'd normally write and there's no trace of your style in it. It's written on your note paper but there's no clue to the person's name who wrote the letter. It wasn't Tony, of that I'm sure, for Tony is a better speller than the chap who wrote under your dictation(?) I'm full of doubts.
>
> What the letter implies is that you're on the ~~point of dying~~, though the words actually used are that you're "leaving the planet." Well, Joey, you're not going to leave the planet, no matter what you do, even you you die and are cremated, for even then the smoke that has been your physical entity won't get out of the precinct of the planet. But hair-splitting aside, let me tell you in so far as I(and probably a few million others) am concerned, you won't be dead, even if you do die. That's why I'm not to be counted among the mourners.
>
> A few weeks ago, Bertrand Mathieu sent me a snapshot of you and him taken six months ago. You look a bit frail in it but still quite alive. You've been through a lot of physical pain and being blind in one eye and deaf in ear is a severe handicap. Yet you seem to have suffered in silence and clung to life. In a way, you remind me of Marshal Tito who died after having for months been on the point of dying. Aren't we all on the point of dying? For months or for years, what's the difference? So in case you do go the way of all flesh ~~I shan't miss you~~ Joey, simply because what's essential in you cannot leave me ever.
>
> So, bon voyage, Joey, and auf Wiedersehen, in Devachan or anywhere else where they decant good vintage wines.
>
> Fred
>
> P.S. Can you give me Tony's address?
>
> Love from Anne

Letter from Alfred Perlès to Henry Miller

> Monsieur Eugène IONESCO
> 96 bd Montparnasse
> 75014 PARIS
>
> Paris le 10 Juin 1980
>
> Madame Barbara KRAFT
> 4369 Camellia Avenue
> Studio City
> LOS ANGELES CALIFORNIA
> 91604 USA
>
> Chère Amie,
>
> Nous sommes rentrés en France depuis bientôt deux semaines, et depuis nous avons été bousculés par des tas de choses, qui ne nous ont pas permis de vous écrire plus tôt.
>
> La mort d'Henry Miller nous a beaucoup touchés, nous l'avions connu chez Buchet/Chastel, ses éditeurs. Nous voulions le remercier des livres que vous nous avez envoyés à Los Angelès: "TRANSIT" et "LE LIVRE DES AMIS". Surtout que dans "TRANSIT" il fait plusieurs fois mention de mes oeuvres. Il y a un mois environ, quand je faisais une signature de livres à la "Southern California", un étudiant m'a apporté un livre et sur la page de garde, était écrit "Alles-y Ionesco" signé Henry Miller.
>
> Il y a deux ans, nous étions dans ce même hôtel que vous connaissez. Henry Miller avait envoyé son chauffeur, mais nous n'étions pas là, il avait laissé son n° de téléphone, mais son infirmière a fait le barrage, et c'est comme cela que nous avons "raté" Henry Miller, et maintenant il est trop tard.
>
> Je voudrais savoir si l'interview qui a été faite, est parue, si oui, envoyez-en moi/un exemplaire.
>
> Nous vous embrassons et espérons vous revoir, soit à Paris, soit à Los Angelès.
>
> Eugène et Rodica IONESCO
>
> PS: Nous avons beaucoup aimé votre étude sur Henry Miller il faut la republier.

Letter from Eugène Ionesco to Barbara Kraft

Translation:
June 10, 1980
Paris

Dear Friend:
We have been back in France for nearly two weeks, and ever since we have been very busy with many things, which prevented us from writing you sooner.

The death of Henry Miller touched us deeply. We knew him through his editors Buchet/Chastel. We would like to thank you for the books that you sent us in Los Angeles, *Transit* and *Livre des Amis*. *Transit* above all, makes several references to my work. It has been about a month since I had a book signing in Southern California. A student brought me a book that had inscribed by Henry Miller on the frontispiece: "Allez-y Ionesco."

It has been two years since we have been in the same hotel that you know. Henry Miller had sent his assistant; however, we were not there. He left his phone number, but his nurse put up a barricade and that is how we missed seeing Henry Miller. Now it's too late.

I would like to know if the interview that took place has been shown and if so, please send me a copy.

We send you a big hug and hope to see you again, either in Paris or in Los Angeles.

Eugène and Rodica Ionesco
PS: We loved your piece on Henry Miller very much. You must republish it.

ABOUT THE AUTHOR

A former reporter for *Time, Washington Post, People, USA Today* and *Architectural Digest*, **Barbara Kraft** is author of *Anaïs Nin: The Last Days, Light between the Shadows: A Conversation With Eugène Ionesco* and *The Restless Spirit: Journal of a Gemini*, with a preface by Anaïs Nin and a laudatory comment by Hemingway biographer Carlos Baker. Kraft's work has appeared in *The Hudson Review, Michigan Quarterly, Canadian Theatre Review* and *Columbia Magazine.* Among the many radio programs she has hosted and produced for the Santa Monica-based NPR station KCRW is *Transforming OC*, a documentary on the 2006 opening of the Renée and Henry Segerstrom Concert Hall in Costa Mesa. Kraft is a Registered Reader at the Huntington Library in San Marino and lives and writes in Los Angeles, California.

Website: www.bkraftpr.com

Contact: Barbara@bkraftpr.com

NOTES

[1] "An Open Letter To Henry Miller": Broadcast over KCRW (National Public Radio), October 2 and 4, 1977; published in *The Noiseless Spider*, a publication of the English Club of the University of New Haven, Spring 1979; Handshake Editions, Paris, France, July 1982.

[2] *The Restless Spirit: Journal of a Gemini* (with an introduction by Anaïs Nin) published by Les Femmes, Millbrae, CA, 1976.

[3] "Hommage à Van Gogh" (*Stroker*, New York, 1979).

[4] "Frau Lou: Dare Everything, Need Nothing": A radio play based on the life of Lou Andreas Salomé (1861-1937) and her relationships with Nietzsche, Freud and Rilke; broadcast over KPFK, May 1974.

[5] Henry received a letter in December 1977 from his friend Béatrice Commengé, who wrote "I've been translating Anaïs Nin's *Erotica* for the last two months—very little of Anaïs in it."

[6] *Anaïs Nin: The Last Days, A Memoir*, ebook edition: Sky Blue Press, 2011; print edition: Pegasus Books, 2013. "Anaïs Nin: Her Last Days"—Article published on Huffpost Arts and Culture:

http://www.huffingtonpost.com/barbara-kraft/anaies-nin-her-last-days_b_1791971.html

[7] My divorce began in the late 1970s at the height of the feminist movement and coincided time-wise with my

meeting Henry; the dissolution of the 19-year marriage was finalized in 1980 after Henry died. I had married at 21 a man 17 years my senior with two small boys, one and three years old. For those years, I had been actively involved in my husband's career, yet I received only seven years' of alimony due to the prejudice against women at that time. The thinking was "since they wanted equality they could go out and get a job and work for it." I had wanted to work during our marriage but my husband had been steadfastly against the idea. Today women once again receive lifetime alimony.

[8] *Big Sur and the Oranges of Hieronymus Bosch*, (New York: New Directions, 1957), pp. 24-25.

[9] According to media sources, Vladimir Putin invited Brenda to visit Moscow as his guest to attend the opening performance of *Venus*, a play about her life.

[10] *Politics of Abortion: An American Entertainment* is a theater piece. The action takes place in a courtroom and centers on the trial of Noelle, a 17-year-old girl charged with performing an illegal abortion—that is, practicing medicine without a license. Having been turned down for a legal abortion by her physician, even though her request was within the legal time period for such a procedure, Noelle goes home and self-aborts the old-fashioned way with a pair of knitting needles. (At present only licensed doctors are allowed to perform abortions in all but seven of the states in the U.S.)

A carnival atmosphere is the prevailing tone of the work. The action takes place in a courtroom set in a circus ring reminiscent of the kind used by old-fashioned European traveling circuses. The raggedy troupe of characters includes the Ringmaster, the Author, Noelle, Henry the Aide, the Mother, the Father, the Lawyer, the Grandmother, the Judge and the Doctor. The Pro-Choice and Pro-Life Representatives are played by the same actor using masks. The Media Two, a male-female TV news team report on the mayhem as it progresses. The Four Greek Chorus Girls double as the Pro-Life and Pro-Choice Crowds. The Ringmaster announces at the beginning of the play that the "subject" would lead one to expect a tragedy but that "when all the parts came together, we saw the comic possibilities were equal to the tragic, running neck to neck as it were." We decided "so much the better...a laugh sheds more light than a tear in these times of moral and social discord."

Near the end of the play the Grandmother dies on stage by dissembling herself—she removes her hearing aid, her false teeth, her eyeglasses, and her heart. Her very existence and her public death are a nuisance to all concerned; no one cares when she dies. The point of her death is to juxtapose this real death of a real human being with the termination of a fetus.

The play has not been produced, but the *Huffington Post* and *Culture Weekly* ran descriptions:

http://www.huffingtonpost.com/barbara-kraft/the-politics-of-abortion_b_1820409.html

http://www.culturalweekly.com/politics-abortion-american-entertainment/

[11] Bertrand Mathieu, a professor at the University of New Haven. Shortly after we met over dinner at Miller's I sent Mathieu my *Open Letter to Henry Miller*, originally broadcast over KCRW in October 1977; Mathieu published it in *The Noiseless Spider* (a publication of the English Club of the University of New Haven where he taught. The piece was also published by *Handshake Editions*, Paris, July 1982.

[12] *Chez Miller*, published in *Stroker*, Summer 1979

[13] According to venerable Jewish legend, one of the "Thirty-Six" (Lamed-Vovnik), living men in each generation, would perform such a surpassing deed of kindness and compassion that God allows the world to go on (e.g., the biblical figure of Abraham). Each remains unaware of his role, and no one can ever identify him. He may be a pauper, a cobbler, a hemstitcher, a seer... Henry said, "I would rather be a Lamed Voynik than President of the U.S., His Holiness, the Pope, or even Muhammad Ali!"

[14] *Anaïs Nin: The Last Days* was published as an eBook by Sky Blue Press in 2011 and in print by Pegasus Books in 2013.

[15] The *Canadian Theatre Review* prefaced the interview, writing, "Romanian-French playwright Eugène Ionesco has not granted many interviews in the course of his long and distinguished career. An extended interview with him is therefore of considerable significance. CTR is therefore pleased to be able to publish the following interview done by Barbara Kraft for National Public

Radio in the United States. Edited for reasons of space, it was conducted this past spring during an international colloquium on Ionesco's work at the University of Southern California. It appears in print for the first time anywhere." Winter 1980. The full interview *The Light Between the Shadows—A Conversation with Eugène Ionesco* was published as an Amazon Kindle book with illustrations in 2014. (See appendix for letter from Ionesco)

[16] G. I. Gurdjieff (1866-1949) was a mystic and spiritual teacher of Armenian/Russian descent. He taught that most humans live their lives in a state of hypnotic "waking sleep" but that it was possible to transcend to a higher state of consciousness and achieve a full human potential. Miller was very fond of his work, including *Boyhood with Gurdjieff* and *Meetings with Remarkable Men*. "Henry Miller: The Last Days"—article on Huffpost Blog:

http://www.huffingtonpost.com/barbara-kraft/henry-miller-the-last-days_b_4454628.html

[17] Music chosen by Miller for his 87th birthday concert and his *Conversation* with me aired over KCRW (the program was re-aired as a centenary concert in Miller's honor on August 1, 1991):

1. Enrico Caruso singing *Vesti la guibba* from Leoncavallo's *Pagliacci* (The Clowns), written in 1892, six months after Miller's birth. The opera was recorded by Caruso in 1907 and he performed it at the Metropolitan

Opera House in New York 89 times. (3 minutes 13 seconds)

2. Cantor Gershon Sirota singing *R'zei*, which means "Accept." Sirota, who was born in Warsaw and perished there in the Holocaust of the Warsaw Ghetto, was considered by many to be the greatest synagogue voice of the 20th century. He came to America on short concert tours, the first being in 1912. He was a tenor, as were Caruso and John McCormack. The song begins "Accept, O Lord our God, Thy people Israel and their prayer..." It is a prayer for the restoration of the Temple service. (3 minutes 45 seconds)

3. *Ondine* from Ravel's *Gaspard de la Nuit* (1908) played by Martha Argerich. Three poems for piano based on poems by Aloysius Betrand, an early 19th century romantic poet. Ondine is a river goddess and the melody Ravel wrote for her rises and falls like the "murmur of a sad voice singing" to quote a line from the poem. (6 minutes 12 seconds)

4. *Swanee River* with Louis Armstrong, trumpet solo. (2 minutes 22 seconds)

5. *Two Sleepy People*, Fats Waller. (3 minutes)

6. Scriabin's *Sonata No. 5 in F-sharp, Op. 53*, played by Ruth Laredo. I think it was the ecstatic quality in Scriabin's music that appealed to Miller. A kind of ecstasy with the cosmos. After four years as a professor at the Moscow Conservatory, Scriabin quit, saying, "I can't bear to hear other people's music all day long and write my own at

night." He went his own way and considered himself at one with the rhythm of the universe. Mystical, original, enigmatic, complicated harmonies, divorced from key relationships. (10 minutes 44 seconds)

7. John McCormack singing *The Garden Where the Praties Grow*. (2 minutes 30 seconds)

8. *Roses of Picardy* sung by Michael Feinstein with Armen Guzelimian at the piano. Part of the old-style Victorian type of sentimental ballad that still lingered in British song writing after WWI. Written by Haydn Wood. (3 minutes 51 seconds)

9. The *Liebestod* from the third act of Wagner's *Tristan und Isolde* sung by Monserrat Caballé with Zubin Mehta and the New York Philharmonic Orchestra. (6 minutes 56 seconds)

www.ingramcontent.com/pod-product-compliance
Lightning Source LLC
Chambersburg PA
CBHW032042090426
42744CB00004B/94